TANGLED ROOTS

Program in Judaic Studies
Brown University
Box 1826
Providence, RI 02912

BROWN JUDAIC STUDIES

Edited by

Mary Gluck
David C. Jacobson
Saul M. Olyan
Rachel Rojanski
Michael L. Satlow
Adam Teller

Number 365
TANGLED ROOTS

by
Israel Bartal

TANGLED ROOTS

THE EMERGENCE OF ISRAELI CULTURE

Israel Bartal

Brown Judaic Studies
Providence, Rhode Island

Library of Congress Cataloging-in-Publication Data

Names: Barṭal, Yiśraʼel, author.
Title: Tangled roots : the emergence of Israeli culture / Israel Bartal.
Other titles: Brown Judaic studies ; no. 365.
Description: Providence, Rhode Island : Brown University, 2020. | Series:
    Brown Judaic studies; 365 | Includes bibliographical references and
    index. | Summary: "In this new book Israel Bartal traces the history of
    modern Hebrew culture prior to the emergence of political Zionism.
    Bartal examines how traditional and modernist ideals and Western and
    non-European cultures merged in an unprecedented encounter between an
    ancient land (Israel) and a multigenerational people (the Jews). As this
    new Hebrew culture was taking shape, the memory of the recent European
    past played a highly influential role in shaping the image of the New
    Hebrew, that mythological hero who was meant to supplant the East
    European exilic Jew"—Provided by publisher.
Identifiers: LCCN 2019059353 (print) | LCCN 2019059354 (ebook) | ISBN
    9781951498726 (paperback) | ISBN 9781951498733 (hardback) | ISBN
    9781951498740 (ebook)
Subjects: LCSH: Jews--Civilization. | Israel--Civilization. |
    Palestine--Civilization.
Classification: LCC DS112 .B3158 2020 (print) | LCC DS112 (ebook) | DDC
    956.94--dc23
LC record available at https://lccn.loc.gov/2019059353
LC ebook record available at https://lccn.loc.gov/2019059354

Printed on acid-free paper.

Contents

Acknowledgments

The chapters of this book draw upon both research and experience. For over half a century I have sought to crack the code of Israeli culture using the tools of the critical historian. But, unlike those of my colleagues who examine distant periods and faraway lands, I study the very culture into which I was born. I experienced this culture's transformations and even took part in shaping it. My parents immigrated to Palestine during the British Mandate from a small town in western Ukraine (then under Polish rule). My mother tongue was Yiddish. The children in the house across the street in our small town near Tel Aviv spoke Polish, Iraqi Arabic, Ladino, and Hungarian. Hebrew was the language of our schooling. I grew up in the heart of the Israeli "melting pot" and, before long, became committed to studying the processes that birthed it. Thanks are due to many individuals whose thinking and scholarship contributed to this book in its present form. Some of my teachers at the Hebrew University of Jerusalem at a time when "Israel Studies" was still considered a kind of "journalism," opened my mind to new understandings of the decisive influence of diasporic Jewish cultures in forging the new culture of the Land of Israel. Jacob Katz, Shmuel Ettinger, and Chone Shmeruk, among the greatest lights of Jewish Studies, raised doubts and posed questions. This book is dedicated to their memory.

Numerous colleagues and partnerships in the study of modern Jewish history have also engaged me in fruitful dialogue over the years, helping shape my interpretation of the wondrous cultural phenomenon that emerged in pre-state Palestine. I mention only two: Prof. Jonathan Frenkel of the Hebrew University and Prof. Yehoshua Kaniel of Bar-Ilan Univeristy. Each, in his own way, was a pathbreaker in the historiography of Israeli society.

Adam Teller of Brown University first suggested presenting the story of Israeli culture to the English-language reader from the perspective of a veteran Israeli historian simultaneously taking an active part in the enterprise of Hebrew culture and conducting critical research into its origins. This was after hearing me lecture at a Slavic studies conference several years ago on the eastern European origins of Hanukkah in its Zionist iteration. In autumn 2013, he invited me to give a series of lectures at Brown, out of which I created this book at Adam's suggestion and under his watchful eye. While transforming the lectures into this book I have enjoyed the support and encouragement of the members of the editorial board of Brown Judaic Studies.

Jeffrey Green and Avery Robinson have taken care to make ancient texts in forgotten tongues accessible to the English reader. They bridged the linguistic and terminological gaps and filled holes in the cultural and historical background. I am also grateful to Maurya Horgan's language editing and Ron Makleff's index preparation and their committed professionalism and willingness to help produce the best book possible.

My grandchildren, Shani, Ayelet, Erez, Naomi, Noga, and Nadav are all children of the twenty-first century. Their forebears came to the Land of Israel from Ukraine, Iraq, and Macedonia, where they spoke Yiddish, Judeo-Arabic, and Ladino, respectively. These boys and girls make up the generation that shall continue the story of the Hebrew culture that developed in the nexus between prophecy, necessity, and spontaneity.

Introduction:
A Culture in the Making

Is there such a thing as Israeli culture? Today, seventy years after the establishment of the State of Israel in 1948, can we really talk about the development of a common culture for an Israeli nation? Would it perhaps be more accurate to speak of a multicultural society that has emerged in the Promised Land—one in which the divisions are more significant than the unifying factors? To find an answer to these questions, we must look at Israeli society from a historical perspective and examine the reciprocal relations that existed between the various Jewish diasporas and the growing Jewish community in the Land of Israel. We must also understand the nature of the power struggle between the new *recommended culture* that the political establishment wanted to establish in the Yishuv and the "old cultures" that continued to exist willy-nilly.

The positions taken by modern Jewish national movements (including Zionism in all its varieties) on questions of culture were, in fact, no different from those of other national movements that arose in modern eastern and central Europe. The Jewish nationalists, just like the Greeks, the Serbs, the Czechs, and the Ukrainians (all neighbors of the Jews in the multiethnic empires of the nineteenth century), truly believed they were reviving an ancient culture. In their view, the heritage of the past that had existed for centuries in religious forms and had been perpetuated for generations in Jewish ritual, contained the germ of a modern national revival. Hence, the nationalist interpretation of the past was conservative and, at the same time, rebellious. Revolt against the old, while preserving it, might seem impossible to an observer unfamiliar with the dialectic of modern national discourse. For the architects of the new national culture, however, it was a powerful tool for enlisting both conservative and innovative supporters.

This duality was, in reality, a direct extension of the Haskalah movement: it was quite common for the same Haskalah thinker, novelist, poet, or historian to become a mouthpiece for nationalist ideas! Decades before the advent of Jewish nationalism, Haskalah had offered the Jews a mixture

1

of Western Enlightenment thought with a closeness to traditional texts that gave rise to an innovative reading of traditional writings. And, as with Haskalah, so with nationalism.[1]

In time, this form of innovative reading itself became an almost sacred tradition. This was certainly the case with the Bible, which the Maskilim in central and eastern Europe regarded as the fundamental text of the renewed Jewish culture rather than the Talmud. This "return" of enlightened European Jewry to the Bible, which took place specifically in the eighteenth century, is unquestionably a result of Protestant Christian influences. Things did not stop there, however. At the end of the nineteenth century, Zionism took the process another step forward by reading the Bible as a historical and political tract, while in contemporary Israel this Book of Books is now regarded as the bedrock of religious-national politics. Few if any people today recall the Maskilic and Zionist approaches to the Bible, which led to its being taught in the secular schools in Israel as an entirely nonreligious text.[2]

The following chapters, which originated as the opening set of lectures in the Brown Judaic Studies lecture series given at Brown University in the autumn of 2013, are case studies in the history of Israeli culture. They deal with the fertile and enriching tension between the programmatic cultural initiatives of the modern age and the premodern cultural forms that continued to exist, sometimes even thrive, on the Jewish street. They offer the reader an unconventional view of the scholarly discourse on Israel, without paying lip service to the kind of liberal apologetics that trivialize the discussion of cultural history and make scholarship the victim of political disputes. On the other hand, they also refuse to submit to the conservative sanctimony that idolizes past cultural unity and avoids confronting the pluralism and complexity of the burgeoning Zionist project.

The reader of these pages will not sense a yearning for any single version of the Jewish past: yearnings of that sort are cultivated by political ideologues of various stripes who tend to use history to serve their own ends. The book does not contain even a hint of the condemnation of the rich

---

1. The Haskalah (secular Jewish enlightenment) movement is generally recognized as originating in eighteenth-century western and central Europe. Adherents are known as Maskilim (singular, Maskil); they advocated for the renaissance of Hebrew into modern life, the study of secular sciences and languages, the participation of Jews in secular society, and the development of the modern Jewish press. See Israel Bartal, *The Jews of Eastern Europe, 1772–1881*, Jewish Culture and Contexts (Philadelphia: University of Pennsylvania Press, 2005), 47–57, 90–101; Shmuel Feiner, *The Jewish Enlightenment*, Jewish Culture and Contexts (Philadelphia: University of Pennsylvania Press, 2004); Olga Litvak, *Haskalah: The Romantic Movement in Judaism*, Key Words in Jewish Studies 3 (New Brunswick, NJ: Rutgers University Press, 2012).

2. On the "secularization" of the Bible by Zionist thinkers, Yishuv educators, and Israeli politicians, see Anita Shapira, "The Bible and Israeli Identity," *AJS Review* 28.1 (2004): 11–41.

cultural creativity that emerged in the Land of Israel—a condemnation that remains popular in much of what is written and said in English in the field of Israel studies. It also contains neither the *schmaltz* of Yiddishkeit nor the anti-Israel demonization so prevalent in the commercial mass media, which shape discourse. Rather, it strives to penetrate the depths of the cultural processes that stood—and still stand—at the heart of the Israeli struggle to maintain a unique cultural identity, which draws upon the inexhaustible resources of the Jewish past and defends itself against the dangers of the present, while continuing to avail itself of the best offered by world culture.

History cannot be separated from politics, especially in a hyperpolitical society such as Israel. Although I know this very well, I have intentionally refrained from using terms prevalent in today's Israeli cultural discourse, such as *Mizrahi*.[3] This is because the labeling of various Israeli ethnic and religious groups has entirely detached discussion of them from their broad historical context and the use of such terms in scholarly writing has been encouraged by their use in Israeli political discussions. Moreover, to the critical historian the present incarnations of ideas, trends, and parties in Israel often appear far distant from what they were just a few decades ago. That is why the terms "right" and "left," as presently used in Israel, have no place in the discussion here. Who, aside from experts in the history of Zionist ideology, remembers today that the Zionist "right," in the spirit of Vladimir Jabotinsky (1880–1940) was identified with atheism, frank secularism, and support for the supremacy of the judiciary in the State of Israel? Equally, who is aware of the depth of the religious sentiment of Aharon David Gordon (1856–1922), one of the most influential thinkers of the "left," the Zionist labor movement? In any event, deep study of the history of Israeli political culture shows that "right" and "left" in Israel have sometimes resembled each other, sometimes mingled with each other, and often overlapped.[4] It is sometimes hard to grasp the value of the simplistic political labeling, frivolously used by politicians, for the work of the historian.

Readers might be surprised by my decision to forgo the classical Israeli-Zionist periodization in this book. Historical discussions of this sort usually begin with the establishment of the Jewish agricultural settlements

---

3. Hebrew for "Eastern" or "Oriental" Jew. Translations of quotations and terms from Hebrew and other languages are my own unless otherwise noted.

4. The case of Joseph Trumpeldor (1880–1920), the Zionist activist and war hero killed in Tel Hai, is a good example of the blurred political identities in the New Yishuv. Both right- and left-wing Zionists regarded this iconic figure as a hero. The Revisionist Zionists named their youth movement Betar, an acronym for "Covenant of Yosef Trumpeldor," while the Socialist-Zionists remember him as a founder of the kibbutz movement. In the same year that he died, the Joseph Trumpeldor Work Battalion (*Gdud ha-avoda*)—a communist-minded labor organization was founded!

after the wave of pogroms that swept the Russian Empire in 1881–1882. I here propose a complete rejection of this periodization in the history of Israeli culture, which has been prevalent for decades in the field of Israel studies.

It is true that the origin of what is called the New Yishuv (or settlements, *ha-yishuv he-ḥadash*) in the history of Jewish society in the Land of Israel lay in the establishment of the first Jewish agricultural settlements in the late nineteenth century. If we are being precise, though, the first two Jewish agricultural settlements to be established in the Land of Israel—Gei-Oni in the Upper Galilee, and Petaḥ Tiqva on the boundary of Judea and Samaria—were in 1878, about four years before the rise of the *Ḥibat Tsiyon* (Love of Zion) movement in eastern Europe.[5] And even this should not hide the fact that, until the first decade of British rule in Palestine, most of the Jews in the country belonged to the Old Yishuv (*ha-yishuv ha-yashan*)! This was the term used for the communities of religiously observant Jews who lived mainly in towns in the Judean Hills and the eastern Galilee, which means that the roots of some contemporary cultural phenomena in Israel lie in developments that took place well before the beginning of the Zionist settlement project.

The historical continuity between the Jews who lived in the country before the nationalist movement and the new settlers at the end of the nineteenth century has been played down for reasons that are primarily political and ideological. Paradoxically enough, that was a point of agreement between those intellectuals, historians, and politicians who were proponents of the Zionist idea and their ideological adversaries, the outspoken opponents of the Jewish national project in the Holy Land. Both cultivated the idea that there had been a break between what had taken place in the Land of Israel during the century prior to the First Aliyah (1881–1903) and what came later. Those who were proponents of the Zionist idea regarded the small religious Jewish community that lived in the Land of Israel as a degenerate branch of the diaspora, fixated on the tombs of the Jewish "saints" and destined to be swallowed up by the waves of national renewal. The opponents of the Jewish national project saw (and still see) the pre-Zionist Jewish community that had lived in the country for many generations, as part of the social and ethnic fabric of Palestine. In their eyes, this community fell victim to the Zionist invaders from Europe who violated the preexisting peaceful symbiosis between Muslims, Christians, and Jews.

Historically speaking, what actually took place in the Land of Israel was far more complex and is reflected in neither of those one-dimensional

---

5. *Ḥibat Tsiyon* (Love of Zion) is a cluster of pre-Zionist associations that were established in 1881–1882 in the Russian Empire as a response to the rise in anti-Jewish pogroms. The movement was officially formalized in 1884 under Leon Pinsker.

scenarios. On the one hand, the cultural processes that shaped the colonies of the First Aliyah cannot fully be understood without taking into consideration the close connections between the Jews of Jerusalem, Safed, and Tiberias and the new settlers in the colonies in Judea and the Galilee. On the other, the Old Yishuv continued to maintain its own way of life, from which some of the new settlers sought to distance themselves, and in doing so substantially impeded the spontaneous processes of change and reduced the influence of those cultural agents propounding the new nationalism.

Three terms will appear throughout the discussion here that seem at first sight very similar, if not synonymous: Jewish, Hebrew, and Israeli. However, these refer to three different cultures that operated in Palestine from the beginning of the nineteenth century and together helped create the Israeli culture we know today. "Jewish" refers to the cultures of the pre-modern ethnic communities established in the country as diaspora outposts, which preserved heterogeneous ethnic and cultural formations that had originated generations before the first Zionist settlement. "Hebrew" (*Ivri*) refers to the innovative culture (or cultures) that the new, ideologically driven intellectual elites in the country wanted to establish. These were sectorial in nature, closely connected to different political parties and movements, and strongly influenced by Western imperial cultures. "Israeli" refers to the culture that arose out of the spontaneous development and growth of individuals and groups—who had either been born in the country or had immigrated from the four corners of the globe—within the Yishuv and later State of Israel. It contains a cluster of adaptations to the local situation, with its colors, voices, odors, climate, foods, and drinks, and became more varied with its contacts with a variety of non-Jewish populations. The Jewish and Hebrew components were born in the diaspora and came to the Land of Israel from outside. There they continued what had begun abroad, mostly in the multiethnic empires where the majority of Jews in the world lived until the mid-twentieth century. By contrast, the Israeli component was dependent solely on the special conditions in the Land of Israel and on direct encounters with its other inhabitants—Jews and non-Jews.

It is impossible to understand what happened in the Land of Israel while the Zionist project was slowly coming to fruition without taking into consideration the great transformations undergone by the Jews of eastern and central Europe in the modern period. Between 1750 and 1914, the conditions of their lives changed fundamentally. First and foremost, almost all the Jewish communities lost the political and sociological infrastructure that had made it possible for them to maintain a traditional way of life. The autonomous community, in which religion and ethnic identity were inseparable—that premodern entity in which the Jews preserved their faith, their laws, and their languages—disappeared. As a result, Jewish cultures that had existed in most places until the nineteenth century within a political and social system that was corporative and feudal, lost their sociological basis. Both in the Russian Empire after the abolition of the *kahal*[6] in 1844, and in the Ottoman Empire after the restoration of the constitution in 1908, the Jews found themselves in centralized states, exposed to the forces of emergent capitalism. Eventually, the rise of the modern state, the full flowering of the capitalist economy, and the appearance of new ideologies exposed the Jews to all the threats and seductions of modernity.[7]

Thus, a decisive factor in the formation of Jewish society in the Land of Israel over the past two centuries has been the crisis of the autonomous, premodern way of life, which has collapsed in the face of external political, economic, and cultural forces. In Palestine, the Old Yishuv managed to maintain a kind of replacement for their previous communities and to preserve premodern Jewish cultures with some success, while the New Yishuv developed some of the ways in which modern Jewry coped with the crisis. It managed to create a new and innovative social infrastructure and, within it, to anchor a nontraditional culture. Thus, in Palestine and later in the State of Israel, different substitutes for the social and cultural structures of the diasporas that had been crushed by the steamroller of modernity existed in parallel, close to each other and distant from each other.

Israeli culture at the beginning of the twenty-first century is without doubt a colossal success story. In my opinion, its success derives from its diversity, from its lack of uniformity, and from the constant subversion of the cultural discourse that aspired to hegemony. It draws upon the cultures of minorities, none of which was able to become predominant in the new country. It is nourished by the democratic power of cultural spontaneity, which introduced outside elements into the trends that the ideologues and political functionaries were trying to control.[8] Its cultural scene is enriched by the continued existence of multiple political narratives

---

6. The *kahal* was the local, corporate governing institution within European Jewish communities that managed internal affairs and was the liaison to non-Jewish authorities.

7. As Rabbi David Ellenson has put it, "When modernity began, the issue for many Jews was 'how do I become modern.' Nowadays there is no problem with being 'modern.' When Jews judge Jewish culture, they judge it in light of values taken from the larger world. And for many a new issue arises—'how do I become Jewish'" (from "How Modernity Changed Judaism," interview with Rabbi David Ellenson, 15 September 2008, Jerusalem Center for Public Affairs, 36, https://jcpa.org/article/how-modernity-changed-judaism-interview-with-rabbi-david-ellenson/).

8. Two recent publications shed new light on the major role of spontaneity in shaping the Israeli culture: Motti Neiger, *Publishers as Culture Mediators: The Cultural History of Hebrew Publishing in Israel (1910–2010)* [Hebrew] (Jerusalem: MN Publishing House, 2017); and Nathan Shahar, *The Songs of Our Youth: What We Sang in the Youth Movement* (Jerusalem: Yad Izhak Ben Zvi, 2018).

within Israeli society, and by the inability of any one, central authority to impose uniformity — even at the height of the statist policy of *mamlakhtiyut* ("statehood") that was pursued by David Ben-Gurion (1886–1973) during the first decades of the independent Israeli state. In addition, it is enriched by the persistence (sometimes invisibly) of various cultural elements brought from across the globe and integrated into the life of the Land of Israel.

Such variety and heterogeneity are generally described as a weakness by both those who oppose the Zionist enterprise and those who claim to be its enthusiastic supporters. In my view, however, this unplanned pluralism is the most impressive chapter in the cultural history of this new nation, which has managed to combine within it a variety of cultures and see itself as simultaneously continuing its heritage and rebelling against it.

1

Pre-Zionist Multiculturalism:
Ashkenazic, Sephardic, and Other Jews
in Ottoman Jerusalem

The one-hundred-year-old Arab–Israeli conflict has led many people to think that the Israeli nation originated with the new Zionist movement. These days few, if any, remember that a considerable number of Jews lived in Palestine hundreds of years before the pioneers of the national movement began the modern settlement project at the end of the nineteenth century. Who remembers that, in the cities of Judea, Samaria, and the Galilee and in several cities along the Mediterranean coast, there were communities of Jewish immigrants who had arrived—some even before the Ottoman conquest of Palestine in 1517—from North Africa, Yemen, the Iberian Peninsula, the German lands, and the Polish-Lithuanian Commonwealth? Who knows—especially nowadays, when the relations between Arabs and Jews are commonly described as a story of prolonged estrangement, alienation, and conflict—about the Jewish, Arabic-speaking communities that lived side by side with Muslim and Christian farmers in the villages of Palestine for many generations? Those Jews, who were called *Musta'aribun* (in Arabic), had lived there since before the First Crusade (1096) and were joined in the following centuries by Spanish and Portuguese Jews who dispersed throughout the Mediterranean basin after the expulsions in 1492 and 1498. In the eighteenth century, the number of eastern European Jews grew steadily. Arriving in groups that sometimes numbered in the hundreds, they settled first in the Galilee, in Safed and Tiberias, and later joined the established communities in Jerusalem and Hebron. Toward the middle of the nineteenth century the Jews in Jerusalem outnumbered all the other religious and ethnic groups in the city.

So, to understand the roots of Israeli culture, we must go back to the annals of the thousand-year-old pre-Zionist Jewish community. The new Jewish national project did not take place in a void; the settlers who arrived in the last decades of the nineteenth century encountered long-established Jewish communities. They had religious, cultural, organizational, political, and economic ties with them and were, to no small degree, influenced

9

by them. To understand that relationship, then, we should examine the social and cultural phenomena that characterized prenational Jewish life, and the best setting for doing that is pre-Zionist Jerusalem—the largest Jewish center in the Land of Israel during the nineteenth century.

A. An Immigrant Community

Jewish society in nineteenth-century Jerusalem was a complex, diverse mosaic of subgroups, whose number and size were constantly in flux. From 1840 on, thousands of Jews from Europe, North Africa, and the Middle East joined the centuries-old community in the city. By 1881, the Jews of Jerusalem were for the most part immigrants or children of immigrants who had lived in the city for no more than a few decades. In this immigrant society, the various groups tended to remain segregated from one another not just on account of their differing social structures and cultural traditions but because the economic system (based on financial support from abroad) perpetuated their separate existence.

The lack of any ideology of unification and integration was typical of the premodern, corporatist character of Jerusalem society. Conversely, the appearance of groups and movements that preached national unity was an unmistakable sign that modernity had come to town. It is no accident that philanthropic agents from abroad, who brought to Jerusalem the ideas of the Enlightenment and its offshoots, took a dim view of the local community's great heterogeneity and did all they could to diminish it, whether in the name of organizational and economic efficiency, Jewish brotherhood, or affiliation with one of the colonial powers. Thus, for instance, the Austrian Jewish philanthropist Ludwig August Frankl (1810–1894), praised the Jerusalem Sephardic congregation for being (in his opinion) a centralized, unifying element and condemned the exaggerated factionalism of the eastern European Jews:

> Their want of union is a further proof of the claims as to the character of Germans [Ashkenazim]; about thirty years ago, they separated from their Sepharedisch [*sic*] co-religionists ... and are now split into six different communities which hate one another.... The word "porisch"[1] means separated; as members of this community, 850 in number, proudly separated themselves from the rest of their co-religionists. They are also called Pharisees.[2]

---

1. *Parush* (Hebrew) or *Porush* (Yiddish) (pl. *Prushim*) was the name of the Ashkenazi non-Hasidic group that emigrated from Lithuania to Palestine in the beginning of the nineteenth century.—IB

2. Ludwig August Frankl, *The Jews in the East*, trans. Patrick Beaton, 2 vols. (London: Hurst & Blackett, 1859), 2:26.

Nonetheless, if one studies the pre-Zionist Jewish community without judging it according to the anachronistic criteria of nationalism and Enlightenment, one finds that this heterogeneity was not a flaw but in fact one of its fundamental characteristics. Its roots are to be sought in the unique historical circumstances in which the Jerusalem community was created as well as in processes common to the development of all the Jewish communities in the Mediterranean basin in the modern era. Deep religious attachment to the Land of Israel and especially to Jerusalem was crucial in drawing to the town immigrants from the various diasporas, shaping their organizational structures, and forging their relationships with their communities of origin.

Immigration to Jerusalem and settlement in the Holy City did not immediately cut off the deep and vital link of these Jews to their countries of origin. On the contrary, since the Jews living in the Land of Israel at that time were very marginal in the spiritual world of the diaspora, they actually needed these connections to continue. One enlightening example of this can be found in the importation of books. For many years, both Sephardic and Ashkenazi Jews had been dependent on the printing houses of Livorno, Warsaw, and Vilnius, until enterprising local printers began marketing books printed in Palestine itself. Yet, even after books began to be produced locally, most of the religious texts used in the country until World War I came from the centers of traditional society abroad.

However, the connection between the immigrants and their descendants and the diaspora was primarily expressed in a two-way movement of people. Emissaries from the Holy Land (Hebrew: *shluhim*) spent years abroad, served as rabbis in diaspora communities, printed their books abroad, and took an active part in religious controversies and polemics in the countries to which they were sent.[3] Fathers whose sons had come of age returned to their native countries to find them suitable matches.

As the means of transportation improved and travel times became shorter, the vibrant relationship between the immigrants and their parent communities grew stronger, as did the organizational-economic ties between donors in the diaspora and Jews residing in the Holy Land. These reached their apogee with the direct involvement in Jewish life in Palestine of organizations in far distant places, such as the communal charity society of Vilnius, the effect of which was to perpetuate the separate character of the subgroups in Jerusalem. Not only did the distribution system rely on the direct relationship between benefactors and beneficiaries;[4] it also meant that there was no incentive whatsoever to leave the group and so forfeit a guaranteed income.

---

3. Abraham Ya'ari, *Shluhey erets Yisra'el* (Emissaries of the Land of Israel) (Jerusalem: Mossad Ha-rav Kook, 1977), 1–143, 569–832.

4. Eliezar Raphael Malachi, *Prakim be-toldot ha-yishuv ha-yashan* (Studies in the History of the Old Yishuv) (Tel Aviv: Hakibbutz hame'uḥad 1971), 98–104.

While this generalization applies primarily to the immigrants from central and eastern Europe, the connection between benefactors and beneficiaries also helped preserve the relationship of the Sephardic immigrant elites with their home communities. In other words, immigrants from the various parts of the Jewish world, who had no desire to integrate with each other, met in the Holy City, lived side by side, and preserved their genetic, economic, and cultural ties to their communities of origin.

B. A Microcosm of the Diaspora?

The relative size and social position of the different groups in Jerusalem changed drastically over the course of the nineteenth century. It is well known that there were almost no Jews there from central or eastern Europe during the period of the Napoleonic Wars, while by the latter decades of the nineteenth century they numbered in the thousands and had gained a great deal of organizational and economic power.

The literature dealing with the Old Yishuv attributes the huge changes in the size of the various components of the city's population to many things, including the destruction of the city of Safed in the 1837 earthquake and the cancellation of the ban on Ashkenazic settlement in the city. In reality, though, the primary reasons for the changes in the size and stratification of the population were social and political developments in the countries of the Jewish diaspora rather than specific events in the Land of Israel. These included (a) the enormous growth in the Jewish population of eastern Europe and the beginning of mass emigration from the region; (b) processes of political change and turmoil in the countries of North Africa; and (c) the organizational and economic crisis in the leading communities of the Ottoman Empire. Taken together, these factors led to the arrival in Palestine of thousands of Jewish immigrants from eastern Europe and North Africa, at precisely the same time that the authority exerted by the Ottoman communities on Jewish society there declined, as did the power exercised by their elites. Alongside this, colonial activities in the countries of the Mediterranean basin grew, and the involvement of the European powers in the affairs of the weakened Ottoman Empire intensified.

The number of eastern European Jews who arrived in Palestine during the nineteenth century was but a drop in the ocean compared to those who emigrated from the lands of the former Polish-Lithuanian Commonwealth to western countries, which suggests that those making for the Holy Land were swimming against the tide of history, so to speak. While hundreds of thousands of Jews were engaging in the processes of industrialization and capitalization in central and eastern Europe or migrating to western Europe and America, a meager few thousand made their way to the East, to regions at the very margins of Europeanization. Even the immigration from North Africa was in part a movement away from Europe and the influence it was having on traditional Jewish society.

Since immigration to Palestine and Jerusalem ran almost directly counter to the major trends in the modern history of the Jews, we must now examine the relationship between the social background of the immigrants and their reasons for immigration. The nineteenth-century waves of immigration to Palestine can be divided into two broad groups. The first consisted of members of the traditional social elites—elderly rabbis and scholars, arriving in groups or individually; the second group comprised the poorest classes of Jewish society. Indeed, the heads of the Sephardic congregation in mid-nineteenth-century Jerusalem protested against the immigration of impoverished multitudes from the countries of the Mediterranean: "For [our] sins, ships are arriving from the west and North Africa [Hebrew: *ma'arav*], from Syria and Arabia, and Turkey and they are all poor and threadbare, barefoot and utterly destitute."[5]

The social elites came to the holy city for religious reasons and followed traditional social patterns. Although instances of marriage between families of elites from different diasporas (such as the marriage ties between the Yellin family from Łomża, Poland, and the Yehuda family from Baghdad) are known, in general the elites perpetuated the existing socioeconomic system that prevented integration, while sustaining a relationship with their society abroad. The lower-class arrivals were part of a much broader Jewish immigration of distress, which became a major phenomenon in the nineteenth century, though only a miniscule part of it found its way to the shores of Palestine and settled in the cities where Jews already lived.

As a result, the subgroups in Jerusalem represented only certain sectors of Jewish society abroad rather than that society in its entirety. They and their families continued to belong to their communities of origin, which lessened their exposure to local changes and strengthened the religious and cultural bonds that connected them. Thus, the immigration of these two groups—the members of the rabbinical elite and the poor Jews—did not contribute to the formation of either a homogeneous or a representative Jewish community in Jerusalem. Moreover, the ethnic mosaic in Jerusalem was not a microcosm of the whole diaspora; rather, it was just a partial aggregation of some of its representatives.

---

5. *Kuntres emet me'erets*, Moses Gaster Ms. 975, 5b, The John Rylands Library, Manchester England, here cited from Meir Wallenstein, "An Insight into the Sephardi Community of Jerusalem" [Hebrew], *Zion* 43 (1978): 75–96, here 87.

C. Europe, Colonialism, Philanthropy, and "Patronage"

The decline in the power of the Sephardi hegemony, which was linked to the weakness of Ottoman rule in the Levant, was a crucial factor in preserving the multiethnic character of the Yishuv. In the eighteenth century, an organization based in the Ottoman capital (the Istanbul Committee of Officials) had administered the affairs of the Jerusalem community,[6] but in the nineteenth century, alternative sources of authority undermined the power of the Jewish leadership outside Palestine and even the position of the government-appointed leader, the Sephardi Chief Rabbi (*Ḥakham bashi*) in Jerusalem.

At the beginning of the nineteenth century all the non-Sephardic Jews in Palestine were still under the patronage of the Judeo-Spanish (or Ladino, Judezmo) community. It took just a few decades for groups of Jews to begin to seek the protection of the consular representatives of the European powers instead. This process took place on the basis of the capitulation agreements that benefitted subjects of foreign powers living in the empire, and it had the effect of removing thousands of Jews from Ottoman jurisdiction, at the same time freeing them from the rule of Sephardic authority. Thus, a triple shift of patronage took place: from that of the Sephardic community to that of a separate Jewish organization (a *kollel*[7] of some sort); from the local patronage of a Muslim potentate, with whom the veteran Sephardic community was in a relationship of dependency, to the protection of a consul of a western power; and from Ottoman rule to the jurisdiction of a European country.

To demonstrate this situation, let us take the case of a Jew who had immigrated to the Holy Land from Lithuania, then part of the Russian Empire, and managed to become a subject of Prussia (the members of the Salomon family in Jerusalem enjoyed such status). From that point on, this person was not subject to Sephardic authority, and his communal life was centered on his *kollel*. If he committed a crime, he was judged in the consul's court according to Prussian law, and if he was harmed by a Muslim, the offender would be punished by order of the consul.

Furthermore, a new Jewish identity, one previously almost unknown in Palestine, was being formed—that of a European subject under the

---

6. Jacob Barnai, *The Jews in Palestine in the Eighteenth Century: Under the Patronage of the Istanbul Committee of Officials for Palestine*, trans. Naomi Goldblum, Judaic Studies Series (Tuscaloosa: University of Alabama Press, 1992), 122–30.

7. This Hebrew word *kollel* (pl. *kollelim*) (in Yiddish: *koylel*) was used in nineteenth-century Palestine in the sense of "subcommunity." New groups of Jews who settled in the land established their own separate *kollel* with their own support system. The *kollel* was the umbrella organization for all their needs.

patronage of a foreign country. There had unquestionably been many such Jews in the cities of the Ottoman Empire as early as the sixteenth century, but in Jerusalem it became a significant phenomenon only in the mid-nineteenth.

European patronage enabled the subgroups of Jews to maintain organizational and economic autonomy. Paradoxically, the European powers allowed the Jews in Jerusalem what they denied to them in their countries of origin: the maintenance, in one form or another, of their premodern, autonomous, corporate existence.[8] In other words, the new European presence in the Ottoman Empire and the increased number of Jews who were becoming subjects of European powers in Jerusalem were also a powerful force preserving the separate identity of the different groups.

On quite a different level, the connection with the various western powers strongly encouraged acculturation, which, when linked to modern Jewish philanthropy, gave rise to the emergence of new *national* Jewish identities in the country.

Such was the case of Ephraim Cohen-Reiss (1863–1943) a Jerusalem-born eastern European Jew who was educated in Germany and England and was, for many years, a central figure in the philanthropic and educational activity of the German-Jewish Aid Society (*Hilfsverein*) in Palestine.[9] Cohen-Reiss was an active agent of German culture, and his educational activity was motivated to no small extent by the desire to compete with the parallel institutions of the Alliance israélite universelle, which disseminated French culture in the Middle East. Clearly, then, the competition between the agents of western countries for the souls of the Jewish residents of Jerusalem also contributed to the maintenance of cultural differences.

Various philanthropic organizations focused their activity on specific sectors of Jewish society in Jerusalem and, as a result, emphasized the differences between them. The activities of the Alliance israélite universelle in Palestine from 1870 to 1914 almost exclusively addressed the Sephardic population. Since its education system flourished in the Mediterranean basin and it recruited teaching staff and principals from the Sephardic and Oriental communities, the Alliance succeeded in creating a cultural connection with Sephardic society that did not embrace the insular, Ashkenazi orthodox groups. The affinity between the communities of origin and

---

8. Israel Bartal, "From 'Kollel' to 'Neighborhood': Revisiting the Pre-Zionist Ashkenazi Community in Nineteenth-Century Palestine," in *Ottoman and Turkish Jewry: Community and Leadership*, ed. Aron Rodrigue, Indiana University Turkish Studies 12 (Bloomington: Indiana University Press, 1992), 203–23.

9. Cohen-Reiss also contributed a great deal to the advancement of modern Hebrew culture in Jerusalem. On him, see Cohen-Reiss, *Mi-zikhronot ish yerushalayim* (Memories of a Son of Jerusalem), 2nd ed. (Jerusalem: Sifriyat ha-yishuv, 1967).

those living in Palestine was also in operation here, so that a Sephardic-French subculture emerged. This, of course, aroused the severe disapproval, not to say contempt, of activists such as Cohen-Reiss, who preferred the German cultural alternative.

The radical young Zionists who arrived in Jerusalem in the early twentieth century saw in the spread of French culture à la Alliance a dangerous process that was corrupting the spirit of the younger generation. In 1911, Rachel Yanait (1886–1979), who later became the wife of the second president of State of Israel, wrote about French education with deep national and socialist conviction: "[It is] the well-known type of Alliance schooling, whose whole educational program and Europeanness is limited to a superficial knowledge of the French language and a poorly ironed uniform. This kind [of education] lacks any moral grounding, spiritual meaning, or basis in life."[10]

On the other side of the spectrum, a zealous, combative orthodox Judaism was coming into being as another manifestation of the direct connection between the communities of origin, in this case Lithuania and Hungary, and the immigrants in the Holy City. It, too, enjoyed the patronage of the foreign consulates in Jerusalem but also battled fiercely against what it saw as concessions on Halakhah (Jewish law) and religious custom. In fact, the Jewish orthodoxy of Jerusalem also seems to have been a clear expression of the penetration of European influence into the East: the orthodox reaction to modernity was a modern European phenomenon, born in a distinctly European context and using European tools to battle against modernizing European influences. Certainly, the transformation of Jerusalem's central and eastern European Jewish communities into an orthodox society created an ever-widening barrier between itself and other parts of Jerusalem society.[11]

While many of the immigrants from Hungary and Lithuania fought the battles of their European brethren against Haskalah and religious reform while creating a fortified, withdrawn community, many of the Sephardic Jews were hearing voices from Europe too—but they were quite different ones as was their response to them. What western-minded writers and visitors from abroad praised as the openness and moderation of the Sephardic Jews in Jerusalem or, conversely condemned as their laxity and cultural weakness, was actually the path that this society took toward Europeanization and modernity.

Though both the cultural trends we have looked at here were very

---

10. Yaakov Shavit, "'Spirit of France' and 'French Culture' in the Jewish Yishuv in Eretz Israel (1882–1914)" [Hebrew], *Cathedra* 62 (1991): 37–53, here 48.

11. "Orthodox" here refers to orthopraxis and not denominational Orthodox Judaism; this usage allows culturally distinct practice (e.g., Hasidic, Lithuanian, German Neo-Orthodox, and Hungarian) to be designated under the singular umbrella of orthodox community.

much part of nineteenth-century European developments, the ways the different communities understood and experienced the European heritage were quite different and made any kind of integration almost impossible. Sephardi society was losing its authority over ever-larger parts of the Jerusalem community and opening up to influences created by the presence of Europeans, while, in contrast, the orthodox community, though splintered into numerous subgroups, was gaining in strength and based its social power primarily on its radical defensive positions.

Orthodox society maintained and strengthened the absolute identity between community of origin and the groups of settlers in Jerusalem by creating a distinct *kollel* for immigrants from each city or district. There was also a tendency to create special quarters for immigrants from different countries or regions. *Batei Ungarn*[12] for Jews from Hungary and the special courtyard for Jews from Galicia exemplify this trend. This style of living made its mark on the historical geography of Jerusalem and permitted decidedly medieval characteristics to continue to exist even as the modern city developed in the twentieth century. Thus, it was specifically thanks to the patronage of the European powers, which encouraged the orthodox to concentrate their social lives on the various *kollelim* and protected them when they did so, that orthodox society was able to wage its battle against modern European culture in Jerusalem.

D. Ideology, Religion, and Nationalism

We have already pointed out that no single element of premodern society in Jerusalem was strong enough to bring about the integration of Jewish society there. While the authority of the established Sephardic community and its official recognition by the Ottoman government had acted as such an element, the size and variety of the new populations that came to the town during the nineteenth century and the strengthening of the presence of the European powers, especially after the period of Egyptian rule in Syria (1831–1840), deepened the differences and heightened the contrasts between the various groups. The overriding trend in the second half of the nineteenth century was toward fragmentation, not organizational unity. Even the North-African (Hebrew: *ma'aravim*; Arabic: *maghrebi*) community, established its own *kollel* in Jerusalem just like the Ashkenazim.

The unifying element that appeared toward the end of the nineteenth century was modern Jewish nationalism. By their very nature, every national movement proclaims the national unity of people who live

---

12. "The Hungarian Houses," an ultra-Orthodox Jerusalem neighborhood established in 1891.

distant from each other as well as members of various subgroups, even those with separate customs and dialects. Little wonder then that, from the very outset, Jewish nationalism argued for the unification of all the different groups of Jews. However, realization of the idea of national unity in a society as complex as that of the Jewish society of Jerusalem, particularly with the lack of any central political force to impose it, was nearly impossible. This was the case even though all the other forces that might have competed with modern Jewish nationalism were much weaker in Jerusalem, for Turkish nationalism emerged very late in the Ottoman provinces and certainly did not take the form of state nationalism.

Taking on a Jewish-Ottoman identity as a political option emerged as a truly influential choice for Jewish intellectuals and public leaders only in the first decade of the twentieth century. Arab nationalism did not appear until toward the end of the period, and British, French, German, and Austro-Hungarian influences competed for the hearts of the students in the various colonial educational institutions (which belonged, of course, to powers that did not govern the land!). On the other hand, a significant faction of Jerusalem's orthodox Ashkenazi Jews had developed an extremely violent antagonism to Jewish nationalism, which they viewed as an unacceptable alternative to the religious view of Jewish settlement in the Holy Land and as a camouflaged extension of the abominated Enlightenment movement.

The nationalist idea, adopted by just a handful of educated Ashkenazi and Sephardic Jews, certainly could not have unified the various ethnicities in the period under discussion here. Nonetheless, it is possible to speak of that handful as the core of a modern elite that bore the message of integration. The political power of the Jewish national movement was to be found not in Jerusalem but in the centers of the New Yishuv, especially in Jaffa. Thus, it came to pass that, for the new movement, the Jews of Jerusalem, like their brethren in the diaspora, were a target for reform and a reservoir of manpower for the establishment of a new society.

Nonetheless, the processes of change that took place in Jerusalemite society as the new city developed and even deep into the twentieth century did little to hinder its continued multiethnicity. The ethnogeographic mosaic of Jerusalem's different neighborhoods preserved the existing character of the city and even strengthened it. Even though supraethnic organizations were established and a modern neighborhood (Zikhron Moshe) built, the new city was, until World War I, fundamentally an intensified version of what had existed before. In the confrontation between the national idea that came from outside and lacked social traction, and the power of established religious custom and cultural difference, the forces of continuity had the upper hand.

E. Cultures Meet, None Dominates

In the culturally diverse setting of nineteenth-century Jerusalem, the connection between the residents of the town and their communities of origin meant that people who lived side by side could belong to different cultural systems separate from the central *kollelim*. The Sephardic Jews shared the culture of the Judeo-Spanish communities of the Balkans, Greece, and Turkey; the Ashkenazi Jews' culture characterized central and eastern European communities; and the Jews of North Africa belonged to quite a different system. And yet they were all engaged in a cultural encounter with one another, whose character was constantly changing.

Who, then, was more powerful? Did the strength of the cultural linguistic system of the Judeo-Spanish speakers predominate at the expense of Yiddish culture? Until the end of the period under discussion here, the separate cultural systems of the immigrants from the various diasporas continued to be stronger than any shared features. And here we must warn the cultural historian against falling into the nationalist trap of anachronism, which emphasizes what is shared over what is unique. No doubt, the very fact of emigration to the Land of Israel, the religious attachment to Jerusalem, and the shared cultural heritage created a common denominator for the immigrants from the various diasporas. As I have emphasized more than once, however, there was no cultural focal point strong enough to unite them.

A difficult and largely unresolved problem that faced the various ethnicities was that of linguistic difference. Even though some scholars maintain that Hebrew (*Ivrit*) served as an interethnic language of communication, the sources show that the members of one ethnicity were unable to understand the Hebrew spoken by members of the others.[13]

It was in response to this linguistic diversity, that the most nationalistic-minded figure in Jerusalem at the end of the nineteenth century, Eliezer Ben-Yehuda (1858–1922), decided that the imposition of a monolinguistic culture was a necessary condition for achieving the goals of the nationalist movement. However, to establish a modernized form of Hebrew as the common language of the Jews in Palestine, it had to be taught to children, and the schools of the different religious and philanthropic

---

13. The following offers a fine illustration of the inability of members of different communities in Palestine to understand each other's vernacular: "The people of the community here [in Haifa] are all *Frenkim* [Sephardim], who don't understand your language, because their language is Arabic and Turkish and Hispanic, and even if you speak to them in the Holy Tongue, no one will understand each other's language, because their accent is different from the Polish" (Menachem Mendl Eilboim, *Erets ha-tsvi* [The Holy Land] [1883; repr., Jerusalem: Ben Zvi Institute 1982], 39).

organizations all taught in the language of their European patrons. The orthodox community fiercely opposed Hebrew-language schools, and traditional educational institutions continued to use the established teaching methods in the spoken languages of the diaspora, including Yiddish, Ladino, and Judeo-Arabic. Thus, neither the European schools nor the traditional ones sought to change the bilingual nature of Jerusalem Jewish society (i.e., a Jewish vernacular and a European language of culture), nor did they propose a single language to unify the entire society of Jerusalem.

As a result, the multilingual nature of Jewish society survived for a long time: the Jews of Jerusalem shared a common language with the diaspora culture to which they belonged and not with their next-door neighbors. For example, in his memoirs, Gad Frumkin (1887–1960) relates that in Jerusalem, the Ashkenazi Jews used to read popular fiction in Yiddish, including the novels of Shomer.[14] Frumkin's father, Israel Dov (1850–1914), was a prolific publisher, editor, and journalist in Jerusalem. For a while he had wanted the distribution of his newspaper, *Havatzelet* (The Lily), to include the entire population of the city, so he published editions in Yiddish and Ladino. Frumkin's brother, Abraham (1872–1946), who grew up in a Yiddish-speaking environment in Jerusalem, moved to eastern Europe, where he became a Jewish socialist and an enthusiastic proponent of Yiddish culture.[15]

Many Jewish families in Jerusalem at the end of the nineteenth century lived linguistic and cultural lives that were similar to that of the Frumkins. These were people in the city who read Hebrew, Yiddish, Ladino, and Judeo-Arabic, but who regarded themselves as part of a large diaspora of Jews who shared their spoken languages. The vernaculars also intermingled, and local dialects emerged, such as Palestinian Yiddish.[16] Thus, the little city in an Ottoman province was a multilingual, demographic, and cultural crossroads, where Jewish ethnic groups on the margins of various diasporas existed side by side, with the constant movement of people, exchange of letters, books, and newspapers between Palestine and their diaspora communities.

These linguistic and cultural differences were but one component of the extremely heterogeneous character of the Jewish population of Jerusalem. Another way in which the differences were expressed was in

---

14. Frumkin, *Derekh shofet bi-Yerushalayim* (Jerusalem: Dvir, 1955), 46. "Shomer" was the pseudonym of Nahum Meir Shaykevitch (1849–1905), a Russian-Jewish author who wrote hundreds of best-selling novels in Yiddish, which were read by Yiddish-speaking Jerusalemites, just as they were read in Warsaw, Vilnius, and New York.

15. In his memoirs, Abraham Frumkin left unique testimony to the unity of the international community of Yiddish speakers in the Middle East, eastern Europe, and the concentrations of new immigrants in western Europe and the United States. See Abraham Frumkin, *In friling fun yidishn sotsyalizm* (New York: A. Frumkin Yubiley Komitet, 1940).

16. Mordechai Kosover, *Arabic Elements in Palestinian Yiddish: The Old Ashkenazic Jewish Community in Palestine, Its History and Its Language* (Jerusalem: Rubin Mass, 1966).

the images that the members of the local subgroups formed of one another. Some of these derived from actual local contact, but others originated from the separate diaspora cultures of the immigrants. On the other hand, the separate groups were brought closer to each other, despite their connections with their separate diasporic cultures, by various social forces, manifestly local in character. These included the shared difference between all the Jews and the non-Jewish environment, as well as their residence in a small and crowded neighborhood (within the walls of the Old City). Yet these forces were negligible compared to the robust combination of economic interest and social positions of power that relied on the center abroad.

While one might expect to find that the massive penetration of European influence was a unifying force, since it appeared to offer a common platform for the members of the various diasporas, that was not the case. As mentioned, each European power had its own constituents, with none enjoying precedence over the others, which created a situation that encouraged the continued existence of separate social bodies among the Jewish population.

The contrast between the various ethnicities in the city was also sharply expressed in one of the most prominent characteristics of modern Jewish history: the varied pace of modernization in the various groups. In Jerusalem, Jews who had been exposed to political reforms of a centralized state and to the innovations of the industrial revolution encountered their brethren who still lived in premodern societies. Since each group retained its affinity with its respective diaspora, its feelings and reactions to the changes of the modern era and the different pace of adapting to them also persisted.

That having been said, the correspondence between European extraction and exposure to the economic, political, and cultural changes identified with Europe was not complete. Certain elites in the cities of the Mediterranean had been exposed to the changes of the modern era long before many of the Jews of eastern Europe. But when the members of the *Prushim* (Lithuanian immigrant) community spoke negatively of the tolerant Sephardic attitude to cultural and educational change, they repeatedly explained it by the fact that the Sephardim had not been exposed to the evils of Europe: radical Enlightenment, political changes, and religious reform.

This image of the openness of the Sephardim in Jerusalem, in contrast to the rigid insularity of the Ashkenazim in resisting the penetration of the influences of western culture is firmly established in the historiography. As the leading Israeli scholar of the Old Yishuv in Jerusalem, Yehoshua Kaniel put it,

> The Ashkenazim who came to Jerusalem to meditate upon the Torah of God day and night opposed the education in the new schools, since the example that stood before their eyes was the Haskalah in Europe and

its grave consequences for Judaism. In contrast, fear of Haskalah was foreign to the Sephardim, and with their practical attitude, they saw no harm in studying languages, especially Arabic, which was the language of the country, or in acquiring other [forms of] secular education.[17]

Since they lacked a powerful internal unifying cultural element, a number of external cultural and social options were available to the Jews of Jerusalem. One was the familiar option of the colonial-era Mediterranean basin: adopting the culture of one of the European powers and identifying with it politically. Another was the local option, which some of the European Jews chose: drawing closer to the Muslim majority population and identifying with the nascent modern Arab nationalism. Then there was the European orthodox option, which favored the preservation of traditional frameworks as far as possible while adapting to the western presence in the city and using its protection as wisely as possible. Finally, there was the option of modern Jewish nationalism, which was by no means strong enough at that time to abolish at a stroke the traditional differences among the ethnicities in the city.

Jerusalem thus resembled several different communities in the Jewish diaspora simultaneously. It had something of the social and cultural situation of Vilnius, in which Jews faced similar options in a multinational and multicultural context, but it was also reminiscent of the situation in Baghdad, whose Jews were making their way toward modernity under the influence of European culture, nascent local nationalism, and a powerful Jewish tradition.

Still, for all their desire to preserve their ties to their original communities abroad, the immigrants to the Holy City, who now found themselves far from the centers of change in the West and on the margins of the colonial efforts in the Mediterranean, were forced to face the toughest enemy of the traditional ethnic-corporatist identity: a modern national movement. It was engaged in establishing a new society out of thin air and demanded the uncompromising integration of members of the various ethnicities as individuals without subgroup identities. This encounter, however, did not alter the character of Jerusalem's Jewish population until the twentieth century, when the other options weakened considerably and the Zionist movement overcame all other social-cultural alternatives.

---

17. Yehoshua Kaniel, "Cultural and Religious Cooperation between the Ashkenazim and the Sephardim in Nineteenth Century Jerusalem" [Hebrew], in *Chapters in the History of the Jewish Community in Jerusalem*, ed. Yehuda Ben-Porat, Ben-Zion Yehoshua, Aharon Kedar (Jerusalem: Ben Zvi Institute 1973), 289–300, here 298.

2

The New Zionist Road Map:
From Old Gravesites to New Settlements

Just a few years after it had begun in the 1880s, the project of Jewish settlement in Palestine, known today as the First Aliyah, had altered the demography and geography of the population in the Holy Land. It had led also to a radical shifting of the coordinates of the imagined map of the country in the Jewish consciousness.

The *religious* map of the Promised Land, on which generations of Jews all over the world had based their ties to that geographic location, no longer matched the new *demographic* map that had emerged following the influx of eastern European and Yemenite immigrants between 1881 and 1903. The Jewish *religious* map of the Land of Israel had been entirely ahistorical, and its relation to the landscape, to the pre-nationalist Jewish communities, and to the extant infrastructure of the real Palestine was tenuous at best. Any correlation between holy places and sites mentioned in the Bible, the Mishnah, and the Talmud Yerushalmi (also known as the Palestinian Talmud) and the actual cities and villages of nineteenth-century Palestine either was made through a Talmudic-halakhic reading of the Bible or was related to a *Ziyarah*, or mystical experience (the term itself is Arabic for a pilgrimage to a holy site). Jewish pilgrims experienced this when they visited the graves of Jewish holy figures in Judea, Samaria, and the Galilee.

Of course, the traditionally accepted pilgrim map had absolutely nothing to do with contemporary modernist aspirations for the social, economic, or political regeneration of Jewish society. It simply mapped routes to the gravesites of the righteous (*tsadikim*) and other pilgrimage sites with no relation to the radical, political worldviews and social programs espoused by some of the new Jewish settlers. No Jewish pilgrim or learned figure of the early nineteenth century had ever believed that the graves of Jewish saints (Hebrew: *qivrei qedoshim*), let alone other sacred places (Hebrew: *meqomot qedoshim*), in any part of the Holy Land, should be considered national sites. Nor would anyone have suggested that such sites might determine the contours of a political entity of some sort. And so it remained until the appearance of modern Jewish nationalism and the trickling down of its ideology into the world of religious beliefs and views, and rites.

The Haskalah movement had, in fact, begun to make changes in the way the map of the Land of Israel was pictured by quite a few European Jews some time earlier. "The transition from focusing upon an idealized Land of Israel—an imaginary country found among the pages of religious texts and the prayer book—to relating to a realistic Land of Israel was part of the Haskalah outlook and left its mark on its literature and other texts."[1]

The new Jewish geographical discourse that had emerged, beginning in the second half the eighteenth century, was influenced by flourishing Western scientific research. European Jews grew even more familiar with the political and social realities of the Middle East during the nineteenth century due to the emergence of the Jewish press. Yet no nationalist-minded or political program had explicitly focused on the map of Palestine before the emergence of the *Ḥibat Tsiyon* movement in the 1880s.

In what follows, I will examine the replacement of the traditional sacred map by the new nationalist map, through the close reading of Jewish travelers' literature. My claim is that these texts give an unequivocal representation of the revolutionary change that occurred in Jewish perceptions of space and time following the beginning of the modern Jewish settlement of Palestine and are yet another example of the cultural shift from a non-European Jewish mind-set to a new Westernized Jewish collective identity. The new geographical conceptualization of Palestine formed one aspect of the emergence of a nationalist identity and so joined the other post-corporative alternatives embraced by millions of Jews in the modern era.[2]

The Holy Land that the new Jewish immigrants and travelers encountered no longer looked to them like a contemporary avatar of the landscapes and places mentioned in the Bible and the Mishnah. In their countries of origin in central and eastern Europe, some of the new settlers had already absorbed a little of the viewpoint of the Western scientist or traveler who had preceded them in the Holy Land. Quite a few of them had adopted the European emotional, national-Romantic discourse from their cultural surroundings. Upon their arrival in Palestine, they wove together what they saw, heard, tasted, and smelled in the villages there into a picture that, though it is possible to discern traditional Jewish hues

---

1. Rehav (Buni) Rubin, *Portraying The Land: Hebrew Maps of the Land of Israel from Rashi to the Early 20th Century* [Hebrew] (Jerusalem: Ben Zvi Institute, 2014), 211.

2. A post-corporative world has fewer geographic and feudal barriers than those historically present in empires, city-states, and other premodern nations. The abolition of the European guild, *kahal*, and other city bodies commensurate with the removal of geographic/legal premodern barriers led to the destruction of the old body politic and its transformation to modern society. See Yair Mintzker, *The Defortification of the German City, 1689–1866* (New York: Cambridge University Press, 2012), 225–55.

in it, was something new and unprecedented in the history of the connection between the Jewish people and the small strip of land nestled between the Mediterranean and the Arabian Desert.

Let us start with a famous map of the Land of Israel's borders (Hebrew: *Ḥalukat erets Yisrael ligvuloteiha*).[3] It is attributed to the R. Elijah son of Solomon (Hebrew: Eliyahu ben Shlomo [1720–1797]), known as the Vilna Gaon, and was first published in Shklov, White Russia, around 1802. It has frequently been reprinted over the last two centuries. The map itself illustrates the attributes of biblical sacred geography as perceived by Ashkenazi pilgrims who visited the Holy Land before the emergence of modern Jewish nationalism. It also represents the way members of the small eastern European Jewish communities in Palestine—Hasidim and/or Lithuanian Talmudic scholars (*Prushim*)—perceived the spatial and temporal context of the Land of Israel.[4]

The Gaon's map had little to do with either Christian Hebraist biblical cartography of the early modern period or the scientific achievements of the time it was designed. Nothing of Jean Baptiste Bourguignon D'Anville's maps of the Holy Land can be found in the Jewish version. D'Anville (1697–1782) was perhaps the most important and prolific cartographer of the eighteenth century and served as geographer to the king of France. As both cartographer and geographer, he reformed the practice of cartography in his day, basing his maps on actual surveys and research that he conducted himself. The results of his work were probably the most accurate and comprehensive maps of his time. He marked a critical point in the history of cartography and opened the way to the English cartographers John Cary, John Thomson, and John Pinkerton in the early nineteenth century. His cartographic project is still considered a major scientific achievement: "It was because of D'Anville's resolve to depict only those features which could be proven to be true that his maps are often said to represent a scientific reformation in cartography."[5]

The map of Palestine to which a link is given here was drawn by D'Anville in 1762 and published in 1794 by Laurie & Whittle, London.[6] It combines state-of-the-art scientific cartography with biblical and post-biblical (including Crusader!) historical geography. In stark contrast,

---

3. National Library of Israel, https://bit.ly/2JHVl5T.

4. Hasidim (sg. Hasid) were followers of the Jewish spiritual revivalist movement begun in the early eighteenth century by the Baal Shem Tov (1698/1700–1760) that was characterized by religious theological alternatives to the dominant traditional Talmudic scholarship common in early modern eastern European communities. The first Hasidic groups settled in the Galilee as early as the 1760s.

5. Thomas Basset and Phillip Porter, "'From the Best Authorities': The Mountains of Kong in the Cartography of West Africa," *Journal of African History* 32.3 (1991): 367–413.

6. "Palestine or the Holy Land in Ancient Times," Wikimedia Commons, https://bit .ly/2V1fNjA.

the Jewish counterpart, by the Vilna Gaon, which was published in the same decade, is schematic and bears only a partial resemblance to geographical reality. Its rivers and streams flow in directions other than their real-life paths: the Jordan, for example, is shown flowing in an impossible direction: from the northeast and, surprisingly enough, simultaneously from the northwest, to the sea of Galilee. The trans-Jordanian Zered stream is shown emptying into the Red Sea, which is placed to the east of the Dead Sea. The Euphrates River flows from east to west, emptying into the Mediterranean.

The Vilna Gaon's map is similar to several other Jewish maps from the early modern period in its close relation to Jewish sacred texts. The Lithuanian scholars who settled in Safed and Jerusalem at the beginning of the nineteenth century had come to the Land of Israel from eastern Europe in order to immerse themselves there in the intensive study of the holy texts. They considered Rabbi Eliyahu ben Shlomo an exemplary figure whom they sought to emulate. So, though they themselves lived in Palestine, these Lithuanian scholars continued to perceive the geography (and the history) of the Holy Land through the double lenses of Talmud and Kabbalah. Their continued use of this map attributed to their revered master is a telling illustration of the gulf that existed between the sacred text and the actual landscape of the Holy Land.

The case of the Gaon's map represents a much wider cultural phenomenon, which had been shared by early modern European Jews for several centuries. Jewish pilgrims, including those who settled in Palestine, saw the landscape mainly through the lens of Jewish postbiblical texts, particularly the corpus of kabbalistic writings that emerged in sixteenth-century Safed. This textual interpretation of places, mountains, and rivers can be described as a kind of geographical midrash. A number of Jewish maps made under the influence of Christian cartographers were published before the Vilna Gaon's map. With one exception, however, printed in Warsaw in 1784, they were all printed to the west of the Polish–Prussian border.

This one exception was rendered by the Polish rabbinic scholar R. Shlomo of Chełm, a well-known Talmudist. He was born in Zamość in 1717 and died in Salonika in 1781, having been successively rabbi of Chełm, Zamość and Lwów. R. Shlomo left Lwów in 1777 with the intention of going to the Holy Land. He spent only a short time in Palestine before setting out for Salonika, where he planned to publish a second volume of his well-known book *Merkevet ha-mishneh*. He never returned to Palestine, dying shortly after his arrival in Salonika. Besides being an authority in rabbinic literature, on which subject he published several works, he was also a talented grammarian and mathematician.

Shlomo of Chełm's manuscript of his book *Ḥug ha-arets* on the geography of the Holy Land was discovered and published only some twenty-five years ago.[7] It contains a map of biblical Palestine,[8] which reveals R. Shlomo's great familiarity with contemporaneous Christian Hebraist cartography. Neither R. Shlomo's map of Palestine, however, nor his geographical work was known in eastern Europe, let alone used by the disciples of the Vilna Gaon, who emigrated to Palestine in the period under discussion.

Returning to the early modern Jewish maps of the Holy Land, those with written descriptions do not seem to have provided practical information for use on pilgrimages. Jewish travel literature, however, does contain some evidence indicating that guidebooks offering itineraries were indeed used by travelers and pilgrims from abroad as well as by Ashkenazi and Sephardic immigrants. Rabbi Moyshe Yerushalmi (Moses the Jerusalemite), for example, who set off on a pilgrimage to the Holy Land in the second half of the eighteenth century (more than a century before the first Zionist colonies were established in Palestine), described the guidebook he used for his journey in the following words (translated from Yiddish):

> In Safed ... there is a beadle who has the book of the holy Kabbalist Our Rabbi Isaac Luria ... who went out and discovered all the gravesites of the Jewish saints and the gravesite of the *tana'im* [early rabbinic Sages] and *amora'im* [later rabbinic Sages] and all the villages and the towns—since, before him, they had all been forgotten—and he marked them. And he himself added what to study while at the grave of each and every *tana* and *amora*, according to the sayings of each, and [he also wrote there] all the prayers to be said when you come to a grave and when you leave it.... So that whoever wants to tour around the Land of Israel and to go to all the graves of the Jewish saints, should first go to Safed, to the beadle, and he should take that beadle with him together with the book. And he should prepare a donkey for [the guide] to ride on and food and drink, and pay the fee for him, since they charge a fee for each and every gravesite.[9]

This mid-eighteenth-century guidebook, described by R. Moyshe Yerushalmi, was evidently one of a series of Hebrew and Yiddish books that were circulated among the Ashkenazi communities in Europe and the Mediterranean in the early modern period. The road map they present combined geography and liturgy, following oral and literary traditions going back several centuries. Of R. Moyshe, who published this description of his tour in 1769 in Yiddish, we know almost nothing. In his text, he made use

---

7. Rehav Rubin, "*Ḥug ha-arets,*" *Aleph* 8 (2008): 131–47.

8. Solomon ben Moses Chelm, *Ḥug ha-arets ha-shalem* (Jerusalem: Mekhon ha-Rav Frank, 1988).

9. "The Travels of R. Moshe Yerushalmi" (originally in Yiddish, 1769), in Abraham Ya'ari, *Travels in the Land of Israel* [Hebrew] (Ramat Gan: Masadah, 1976), 424–59, here 430–31.

of previous travel books and incorporated some information he himself had gathered on a visit to the Galilee. The main part of his book consists of a description of two pilgrimage routes—one short, one long—for visiting holy sites in the Holy Land. He identifies geographic locations through the use of both the ancient Talmudic text and much later kabbalistic traditions. He also, however, updated the descriptions with observations that he himself had made in Safed, Tiberias, and the surrounding regions. The writer describes his book as "a description of the villages and towns and the holy graves of the righteous [*tsadikim*] and pious ones [*hasidim*] in the Land of Israel."[10] It also contains a list of sites in and around Safed, Tiberias, Jerusalem, and Hebron that are quite similar to those in Jewish travel books of previous centuries.

Comparing the route taken by R. Moyshe Yerushalmi in eighteenth-century Palestine with that of a visit made some 120 years later by another Jewish traveler from eastern Europe, Mordechai ben Hillel Hacohen (1856–1936), clearly shows that a profound transformation had taken place in the geographic conception of the Land of Israel. Its roots can be traced back to the founding of the first modern Jewish agricultural colonies (*moshavot*; sg. *moshava*) in 1880s Palestine. Hacohen was one of the founders of the *Hibat Tsiyon* movement (Love of Zion)—a forerunner of modern Jewish nationalism in the Russian Empire—and he made two visits to the Land of Israel, in 1889 and 1891, during the period of the First Aliyah. Unlike his predecessor, Mordecai ben Hillel Hacohen was steeped in the ideology of modern nationalism mixed with European Enlightenment thought. Furthermore, he had social and political aspirations the likes of which had been rare in traditional Jewish circles. He was also a businessperson, an entrepreneur who observed the country from an economic perspective.[11]

This early Zionist pilgrim was one of the first in a series of dozens of travelers who replaced the accepted, sacred itinerary with a new, nationalist one. Hacohen, who landed at the port of Jaffa in 1889, describes the route he chose for his journey in the following words:

> I plotted myself a route from Jaffa to Rishon Lezion, from there to Gedera, Nahalat Reuben or Wadi Hanin, and then to Be'er Tuvia or Kastina, and back to Gedera. From there [I would go] to Ekron, and then via Rishon Lezion to Petah Tiqva and Yehud, and afterwards to Jerusalem. From Jerusalem [I would travel] to Nablus, Tiberias, Safed, Rosh Pina, Yesod

---

10. Haim Goren, "An Eighteenth-Century Geography: Sefer Yedei Moshe by Rabbi Moshe Yerushalmi" [Hebrew], *Cathedra* 34 (1985): 75–96, here 78.

11. On Hacohen's political and literary career, see his memoires: *Olami* (My World), 5 vols. (Jerusalem: Worker's Press, 1927–1929).

Hama'ala, and then back to Rosh Pina and on to Haifa by way of Peki'in, the colony of Jews who have been inhabitants of the land from ancient times [and] who speak only Arabic. From Haifa [I would go] to Zikhron Ya'akov, and from there back to Jaffa.[12]

What is common to both the old and the new routes of the Jewish travelers is that the starting points were in towns where the pre-Zionist Jewish communities existed. In the first case, however, the towns themselves, Jerusalem, Safed, Tiberias, and Haifa, were of secondary importance to the clusters of gravesites scattered about in the countryside around them. The nationalist-minded itinerary, on the other hand, replaced the traditional pilgrimage sites with the new agricultural colonies (founded only a few years previously). Moreover, the new settlements, which were situated near the cities, were now thought by the travelers to radiate something of the spirit of the new era back onto the old communities.

The new Jews of the colonies functioned here as both the objects and the subjects of Zionist travel. In Hacohen's mind, they gave new meaning to the role of the towns of the Old Yishuv in the nation's history and the country's geography and, in so doing, redrew the map of the Holy Land. This is what Mordechai ben Hillel Hacohen wrote in his travelogue about Jerusalem:

> The ornament and eternal [nature] of Jerusalem will ennoble the new colonies and their inhabitants with its spirit. Their holy city is close to our brothers who reside in the Land of Judea and they sense that Jerusalem is the heart of Israel, the heart of the entire people. The new [Jewish] peasants now feel the movement when the city of Zion sways, and they lend an attentive ear to everything happening in Jerusalem. On the festivals, the peasants go up to Jerusalem, they fraternize with and get to know these 'modern people.'… That is the power of Jerusalem over the colonies.…
>
> On the other hand, the reverse [is also true]. The colonies will also have a great influence on the Judean hills region, first and foremost, Zion [i.e., Jerusalem]. The colonies of our brothers, those who till the land, are a living example to the dear inhabitants of Zion, that the Land of Israel was not created in vain, for Jews to walk there idly all the day and to eat the bread of idleness without the labor of the hands. It is the mission of Israel in its Land to till it and to tend it. What was given [to] us was a desirable, good, and spacious country, not a house of worship and a place of assembly for the old.[13]

---

12. "Travels of Mordechai ben Hillel Hacohen (1889)," cited here from Ya'ari, *Travels in the Land of Israel*, 651–707, here 654–55.

13. Ibid., 696–97.

Dozens of Jewish travelers took the new route that replaced the pre-Zionist itinerary and described the new nationalist pilgrimage in a wide variety of publications in Hebrew, Yiddish, Russian, and German.[14]

The new geography that emerges from the route taken by the nationalist-minded travelers, members of the *Ḥibat Tsiyon* movement, did not change its focal points only from the perspective of *place*. It also linked itself to a new *time*: a time of nationalism, Western time, a new era for social repair (*tikkun* — an old mystical concept in a new secular meaning). This can be seen in the sharp words Mordechai ben Hillel Hacohen used against the Old Settlement (*ha-yishuv ha-yashan*) — a Hebrew term already used in the years of the First Aliyah to refer to the pre-Zionist Jewish communities in the towns of Palestine. His criticism of the ahistorical nature of the pre-Zionist Jews' relations with the land of their ancestors was no less biting: for him it was a bond expressed through the cult of holy places.

Describing his visit to Hebron, Moredechai ben Hillel told how local Jews brought him to the graves of the biblical Avner ben Ner and Otniel ben Kenaz. His guides also showed him the place where Abraham the Patriarch received his three guests (see Genesis 18:1–15). The historically minded traveler derided his guides' attachment to the place as based only in legend and also complained about their ignorance of the city's history: "All the other things shown to visitors in the city Hebron are just the same — superstitious legends. But even those who deny [their historicity] do not realize how the town [i.e., Hebron] has experienced numerous events and has developed [as a result of] varying circumstances."[15]

Until the late nineteenth century, the Jewish geography of the real-life Land of Israel was concentrated in four regions of urban settlement: two in the Galilee (Safed and Tiberias) and two in the Judean hills (Jerusalem and Hebron). Other Jewish settlements that had existed in the seventeenth and eighteenth centuries, such as those in Gaza and Nablus, had dwindled into insignificance by the time of the First Aliyah. In fact, before the establishment of the new *moshavot* in Palestine, the small Jewish community there numbered less than thirty thousand people in 1880 and was almost entirely situated deep in the mountain areas of Palestine. Even the limited economic activity that began to develop in the coastal cities (mostly Jaffa and Haifa) beginning in the 1830s had not attracted more than a few hundred Jewish residents by the 1870s.

Thus it was that the establishment of the new *moshavot* on the coastal plain and in the area around Haifa, shifted the demographic center of gravity from the pre-Zionist Jewish community in the inner hill country to the Mediterranean coast. The shift also reflected economic developments,

---

14. The most well known of those publications was Ahad Ha'am's (Asher Ginsberg) *Emet me-Erets-Yisrael* (A Truth from the Land of Israel, 1891). For a partial list of this new nationalist pilgrimage literature, see Ya'ari, *Travels in the Land of Israel*, 782–83.

15. Ya'ari, *Travels in the Land of Israel*, 691–92.

most notably the creation of commercial and business centers around Palestine's western ports. It was a reversal of profound importance that reflected the strengthening of economic ties between Palestine and Europe. The new nationalist travelers observed the direct connection of the new settlement enterprise to these economic changes: in their minds, Jewish nationalism was bound up with European technology, modern industry, and commercial prosperity.

This can be seen in the writing of David Yudelovitch (1863–1953), another member of the young nationalist movement, who lived in Rishon Lezion in the early years of the new Jewish settlements. He wrote one of the first books in Hebrew on economic activity in the Land of Israel, identifying the agricultural colonies with modern forms of entrepreneurship. For him, the geographic shift from the backward mountain area to the outskirts of the two developing port towns of western Palestine signified the opening of the modern Jewish community to European influences and the colonies' geographic proximity to either Jaffa (which he termed the "source of Israel's commerce and profit")[16] or Haifa was of vital importance.

Yudelovitch well understood that, commercially speaking, the Jewish national project would benefit from linking the new colonies to international commercial centers. Hence, his descriptions of the newly established sites on the national travel itinerary sound highly Orientalist to contemporary ears. His views were indeed decidedly Western: Palestine's development was lagging due to the nature of its Oriental inhabitants— including traditionally oriented Jews from eastern Europe. The new residents of the colonies, unlike their coreligionists in the old cities of Palestine, however, had adopted the ways of the West. In the Land of Israel, these new immigrants from eastern Europe were continuing the dream of the Haskalah to Westernize the Jews. The description of the *moshavot* in Yudelovitch's book supplemented his economic vision, which revolved entirely around entrepreneurship, the circulation of capital, trade and industry, as well as a cultural and spiritual receptiveness to the West:

> There is no profession in the Land of Israel that cannot be considered ready to enjoy the benefits of the modern settlement, and there is no corner to be found that does not feel the need for an expanding industry. Achieving this, demands, however, industrious and knowledgeable people and diligent and busy hands [to] lift [the land] out of its degradation, to strengthen its position, to improve and beautify it.... For through slothfulness, ceilings will sag, and fertile lands will turn into a salt marsh, [all] because of the idleness of its inhabitants. Six years have not yet passed from the time when gazelles rested peacefully in the *Eyn Hakore* [Ayun

---

16. David Yudelovitch, *Sefer ha-mishar veḥaroshet ha-ma'aseh be'erets Yisrael* (Warsaw: 1890), 51.

Kara] wilderness, and jackals prowled there; today it has become the colony of "Rishon Lezion": the wilderness has turned into [the Garden of
Eden], the desert into a vineyard.... Five years ago, the environment at
Shimron Meron [Zamarin] was just cracks in the bedrock and copper-like
earth; today it has become Zikhron Ya'akov, a Valley of Blessing where
the People of Israel live from the fruit of the land and [their] industry and
labor.... These several places serve us as an example of what patience and
industry and diligent hands [can] achieve.[17]

In sum, within less than a decade (1882–1889), the map of Jewish settlement in Palestine had changed. A group of Jewish colonies had been
established on the coastal plain, in the hills southeast of Haifa, and in eastern Upper Galilee near Safed, making an unprecedented addition to the
old clusters of Jewish population in Palestine and altering the spatial
spread of the communities. This was not only a demographic shift: the
First Aliyah changed basic Jewish conceptions of *place* and *time* in the Holy
Land.

This was connected not just with the economic innovations and the
cultural developments undertaken by the new settlers. The settlement
project itself, aimed as it was at regenerating the *Ostjuden*,[18] was yet
another Western challenge to both the culture and the socioeconomic
character of the long-established Old Yishuv. Moving the eastern European immigrants into so-called productive occupations and changing
their professions from petty commerce and the like to agriculture, crafts,
and industry, through the establishment of the colonies, caused a radical,
if not revolutionary change to the map of the Holy Land. To the nationalist-
minded visitors, the newly founded villages seemed to be part of a different place—the West—and a new era— that of the national revival. Thus it
was that the modern nationalist map of the Land of Israel replaced the
traditional sacred one.

This transformation fits some of the observations made by Eyal
Chowers (b. 1959) in his book *The Political Philosophy of Zionism:*

The third temporal imagination of modernity identifies this epoch as
essentially present-centered, and it was significant for the rise of Zionism: it involved a view of human life as less bound by tradition and
authority and saw the concerns of the concrete, living Jew as the par-
amount consideration for how individual and collective action should
be shaped. As did other Europeans, Jews began to see time as a limited
resource that could be crafted by human endeavor and be used in bene-
ficial ways; moreover, the present was in a sense the realm of freedom—

17. Ibid., 14–15.
18. *Ostjuden* is a German pejorative term for the "Eastern Jews," a Yiddish-speaking
Jew who immigrated to Germany and Austria but also into other "German" spaces.

unfettered by the past, not chained to a meta-narrative and a binding future.[19] In daily life, Jews (especially in western and central Europe), were increasingly inclined to limit the time devoted to prayers and the study of ancient texts to communal events, ceremonies, and practices (such as the *mikve*). Instead, modern Jews tended to utilize time carefully, devoting more of it to the economic sphere and the cultural one (that is, in the spirit of *Bildung* [education]). This activist and matter-of-fact attitude toward time was conducive to the determination of Zionists to take history into their own hands; for the Zionist individual, time became a religiously neutral resource open to an ethos of initiative and shaped by the modern's cultivated imagination.[20]

It should be said, however, that, despite its new and unprecedented relation to the geographical reality of Palestine, the nationalist map that emerged in the late nineteenth century did not contain only obviously modernistic elements. It also gave clear expression to the desire to avoid the dangers of modernity. An ambivalent attitude toward both the old and the new sites connected the First Aliyah itineraries to the traditional Jewish ones. The Western-minded nationalist traveler included in his newly planned route some of the old places. However, instead of taking part in traditional religious rituals when he visited them, he transformed them into new national sites of memory. In Hacohen's travelogue, Jewish mysticism gave way to history, and rabbinic scholarship was read in a European "scientific" mode. In that way, the new Zionist road map managed to embrace at least some aspects of the pre-Zionist pilgrimage to the Land of Israel.

---

19. This is in contrast to the "passive" mode of Jewish messianism attributed by early Zionist thinkers to orthodox Judaism. —IB.

20. Eyal Chowers, *The Political Philosophy of Zionism: Trading Jewish Words for a Hebraic Land* (Cambridge: Cambridge University Press, 2012), 60–61.

3

Imperial Identities:
Nationalism, Politics, and Culture

In the Jewish year 5642 (1881 CE), almost 140 years ago, the first immigrants of what would subsequently be called the First Aliyah reached the shores of Palestine. Jews from cities and towns in Romania, which had been under Ottoman rule until four years earlier, settled in two farming colonies that bordered on two Arab villages: Rosh Pina (next to Ja'une, on the eastern slopes of the hills of Safed) and Zikhron Ya'akov (at Zamarin village, on the southern flank of the Carmel range). In doing so, they laid the foundations of the New Yishuv, the new community of Jewish immigrants who would go on to create on the eastern coast of the Mediterranean a culture unprecedented in Jewish history. It was a secular Hebrew culture that was a rebellion against the traditional world while at the same remaining faithful to some of its values.[1]

Were the course of history plotted by ideas alone, one would expect the Land of the Patriarchs to have given rise to an exemplary culture in the spirit of the eastern European Jewish Enlightenment movement: a merger, so to speak, of the legacy of the eastern European version of Ashkenazi culture and the cultures of western Europe. That is perhaps what would have developed, had the new settlers possessed a clear and consensual vision of the future of Jewish culture in Palestine. However, no such vision existed. Furthermore, from the very dawn of the modern Jewish national movement, the issue of culture had been at the root of vehement disputes. The national Orthodox pulled in one direction, while the so-called free nationalists pulled in others.

---

1. The first group of settlers to promote a blunt secular version of Jewish identity in 1880s Palestine was *Bilu*. Its members came from the Russian Empire in 1882 and established the farming colony Gedera (1884). For a discussion of its origins and impact on other Zionist settlement movements, see Shulamit Laskov, *Ha-Bilu'yim* (Tel Aviv: Ha-sifriyah ha-tzionit, 1989); Jonathan Frankel, *Prophecy and Politics, Socialism, Nationalism and the Russian Jews, 1862–1917* (New York: Cambridge University Press, 1981), 90–97; Israel Bartal, "Farming the Land on Three Continents: Bilu, Am Oylom, and Yefe-Nahar," *Jewish History* 21 (2007): 249–61.

However, the controversies over the future direction of the new culture were not the only cause of the steadily widening gap between the different cultural aspirations and the situation on the ground in Palestine. The culture itself—or, to be more precise, the cultural baggage that the new settlers brought with them—also had a decisive influence.

The seeds of modern Palestinian-Jewish multiculturalism were sown in the very first year of the first wave of immigration (1881), and the new amalgam persisted and flourished under the ideological mantle that various functionaries, writers, teachers, and other agents of culture threw over it. In 1882, it was not only Yiddish-speaking settlers from the *shtetlekh* of northeastern Romania—a border zone between Imperial Russia and the Ottoman Empire—that reached Palestine. Arabic-speaking immigrants from Yemen arrived, too, settling in Jerusalem.[2] Others also arrived from various provinces of Imperial Russia to establish villages in Judea and the Galilee.

Each group came with its own culture. A jumble of immigrants, a babel of languages, and a range of religious traditions soon filled the land. Yiddish-speaking Hasidim from Poland and Sephardim from Anatolia lived side by side. Both had to submit to the discipline of the so-called clerks (administrators) of Baron Edmond de Rothschild, who were imbued with the French culture they had acquired as alumni of the Alliance israélite universelle education system in the Ottoman Empire or the communities of northern Africa.[3] The rabbis of the Old Yishuv—nearly all products of communities in Imperial Russia and the Austro-Hungarian Empire—were not strangers to the agricultural colonies. Strong ties bound the Jews of Jerusalem, Safed, and Tiberias to the new farmers. The Muslim fellahin, among whom the first new villagers made their homes, lived in the courtyards of the Jews' farms, their children played with those of the settlers, and the Palestinian Arabic vernacular was heard in the village streets, the vineyards, the almond plantations, and the citrus groves. The schools in most of the villages taught French. Yiddish was spoken at home and Arabic on the farm.

All these influences were countered by a small group of intellectuals—teachers, writers, newspaper editors—brimming with national consciousness. Their idea was to guide the march of civilization toward the creation of what they envisioned as a Hebrew culture. The story of the new Israeli culture thus began with this confrontation between spontaneous processes of growth and attempts to shape them. Later on, in the British Mandate era, the modernist political movements gathered strength

---

2. On the Yemenite Aliyah in the years 1881–1894, see Nitza Druyan, *Without a Magic Carpet* [Hebrew] (Jerusalem: Ben Zvi Institute, 1982).

3. For the French orientation of the baron's administration, see Ran Aaronsohn, *Rothschild and Early Jewish Colonization in Palestine* (Lanham, MD: Rowman & Littlefield, 2000).

in the Jewish community, the nexus of ideology and culture was culti-vated, and organizational systems that amplified the strength of the guided culture emerged. The new Hebrew culture blossomed, diversified, and acquired status and prestige.

However, even as the organs of the new culture such as the national school systems, the Hebrew University of Jerusalem, book publishers, newspaper editorial boards, and the Hebrew radio grew to peak strength, long-term spontaneous processes continued to be drawn into the forma-tion of the guided culture. The sundry vernaculars that were current in Palestine in the mass immigration years penetrated the Hebrew language as it regenerated, leaving distinct impressions. Mediterranean locutions blended into those of eastern Europe; the immigrants accepted various modes of dress and menu items that had no ideological justification. The new Hebrew culture that arose in Palestine was the outgrowth of a com-plex and multifaceted interplay between spontaneity and demography, on the one hand, and ideology and politics, on the other.

In the State of Israel's early years—the salad days of what the Israeli sociologist Oz Almog calls, using a slightly antiquated term, "sabra cul-ture"[4]—members of the socialist Zionist youth movements eagerly read a slender publication called *Yalqut ha-kezavim* (literally, "The Bag of Lies," or "The Collection of Falsehoods").[5] This book, an assortment of tales and sayings that were current among members of the Palmach—the com-mando unit of the Haganah in the 1940s—was presented by its editors as one that could be understood only by "those who walked the dusty roads of the years 1942–1948 and drank strong coffee from used tin food cans around campfires."[6]

For the critical reader, though, *Yalqut ha-kezavim* sheds light on some of the hidden roots of Israel's cultures. In what follows, I will use two stories from this collection to give us some insight into the formation of Israel's sociocultural reality.

Four cultures are alluded to in the two *kezavim* (stories):

1. The pre-modern Jewish culture (or, to be more precise, cultures)
2. The local Palestinian culture

---

4. Oz Almog, *The Sabra: The Creation of the New Jew*, The S. Mark Taper Impring in Jew-ish Studies (Berkeley: University of Califronia Press, 2000), 22.

5. Dan Ben-Amotz and Hayim Hefer, eds., *Yalqut hakezavim* (Bag of Lies) (Tel Aviv: Ha-kibbutz ha-me'uhad, 1956); Ben-Amotz and Hefer, eds., *Yalqut hakezavim hamale ve-hashalem* (The Complete and Unabridged Bag of Lies) (Tel Aviv: Metsi'ot, 1979); Ben-Amotz and Hefer, eds., *Yalqut ha-kezavim, mahadura mehudeshet, mueret umevoeret* (The Annotated Complete and Unabridged Bag of Lies) (Tel Aviv: Kinnereth, Zmora-Bitan, Dvir Publishing House, and Aryeh Nir Publishers, 2009).

6. Michael Keren, "Commemoration and National Identity: A Comparison between the Making of the Anzac and the Palmach Legends," *Israel Studies Forum* 19.3 (2004): 9–27, here 22.

3. The imperial cultures with which the Jews had bonded in the modern era, either in Europe or in the Mediterranean communities that were exposed to the cultures of the colonial powers
4. The new Hebrew culture on which a new Palestine-born generation had been raised

The vignettes in *Yalqut ha-kezavim* seem to contain a kernel of truth when they describe the cultures that influenced society in Palestine, both Jewish and Arab. The first was based on events that took place in the 1940s under the British Mandate. It ostensibly documents the way of life in the Jewish village of Metulla, close to the Lebanese border of British Palestine. At that time, Lebanon was ruled by the declining French colonial empire, and Jews from Syria and Lebanon were entering Palestine from there illegally. These immigrants were called in Hebrew *ma'apilim* (the biblical term for the Israelites who proposed to enter the Promised Land from Sinai, against Moses's instructions). Metulla, the northernmost Jewish locality in British Palestine, is a *moshava* that was founded in 1896 by participants in the First Aliyah in a Druze village whose inhabitants were forcibly displaced to Syria by the new legal owners of the lands.

In the vignette, a group of young Jews born in Palestine, who served in the Palmach, led the immigrants from the French side of the border to the British. It did not take long before the Palmachniks found themselves in the vicinity of Metulla, even then a veteran Galilean village. One of them turned to a farmer from Metulla who was plowing his fruit orchard and asked him in vernacular Hebrew: "Excuse me, please, might I possibly have some water?" The farmer summoned his Arab worker and asked him in Yiddish, "Mukhamed! What did he say [*Vos zogt er*]?"[7]

The second anecdote conveys something of the cultural reality of Nahalal, a cooperative farming village established during the Third Aliyah (1919–1923), only about twenty years before the incident reported in *Yalqut hakezavim* was supposed to have happened. An "old" woman from Nahalal (judging by the history of Nahalal, she must have been around fifty) saw Micah the Palmachnik "returning from the field, his clothes a little mussed. 'When I was young,' she told him, 'it was all different. When a couple went out for a walk, they talked about Pushkin, Dostoevsky, and Lermontov. Today, I see, they go straight to the *goyel nefesh*" (the "disgusting thing"). What is important for us is that she spoke the Hebrew words with a Yiddish inflection.[8]

These two stories, almost nonchalantly, evoke the roots of Israel's new culture but at the same time give expression to the four cultures mentioned above, showing us how they interacted. The use of Yiddish in both

---

7. Ben-Amotz and Hefer, *Bag of Lies* (1956), 37.
8. Ibid., 107.

tales reveals the presence in Palestine of one of the premodern cultures of Jewish society, which had persisted in the multinational empires of central and eastern Europe and ridden the coattails of the first Aliyot (post-1880 waves of immigration) to the Galilean village and the Jezreel Valley farming cooperative. Arabic, the local native tongue, was absorbed by the Jewish colonies of the First Aliyah era together with other local cultural elements such as food and clothing.[9] The woman from Nahalal, who spoke Hebrew peppered with Yiddish, had brought to the Jezreel Valley a non-Jewish high culture, which the Jews of the Pale of Settlement, on the periphery of Imperial Russia, had absorbed. She reflects something of the Jews' acculturation in the Imperial Russia of the late nineteenth and early twentieth centuries. She might not actually have read anything by Dostoevsky, but, like thousands of her age group who had been born in the *shtetlekh* of the western provinces of Imperial Russia, she belonged to the first generation that had imbibed the imperial culture. She knew full well that high culture—even in the little Mediterranean land that she had reached, inspired by grand ideas of reforming the world and bringing on the Jewish redemption—meant that Dostoevsky should be mentioned, and that Pushkin's poetry should be quoted during the courting ritual of civilized people. But Palestine, of course, already had a new culture, nurtured by the new Hebrew education system and empowered by the Zionist youth movements—a culture of which the stories told by the Palmachniks, speakers of the resurgent Hebrew language, were also a part.

What were the cultural features of the tiny Jewish population that had settled in Palestine before the onset of the new settlement movement in the late nineteenth century? In the early modern period, three main premodern Jewish cultural diasporas sent offshoots to Palestine. The first of these diasporas was that of Ashkenazi Jews from the communities of central and eastern Europe. When they settled in Palestine, they encountered members of the Sephardi and Mediterranean diasporas, who had come into contact with the local culture—that of the indigenous non-Jewish population, nearly all Arabic-speaking. The Sephardi Jews, whose Jewish vernacular was Ladino (Judeo-Spanish/Judezmo), had lived in Palestine for centuries, had become part of the country's landscape, and had imbibed its traditions. There were also Arabic-speaking Jews in Palestine, known as *Musta'aribun.* They lived in various Galilean villages and were regarded with passionate admiration by some of the Zionist immigrants

---

9. On the Yishuv in its Arabic-speaking context, see Liora Halperin, *Babel in Zion: Jews, Nationalism, and Language Diversity in Palestine, 1920–1948* (New Haven: Yale University Press, 2014), 142–80; Israel Bartal, "Hanukkah Cossack Style: Zaporozhian Warriors and Zionist Popular Culture (1904–1918)," in *Stories of Khmelnytsky: Competing Literary Legacies of the 1648 Ukrainian Cossack Uprising,* ed. Amelia Glaser, Stanford Studies on Central and Eastern Europe (Stanford: Stanford University Press, 2015), 139–52.

from eastern Europe during the first national Aliyot. Thus, three main cultures and their offshoots sank roots in the towns of Palestine between the sixteenth and nineteenth centuries: (1) "Oriental" Jewish culture;[10] (2) Sephardi culture; (3) Ashkenazi culture.

A general overview of the Jewish world in the late eighteenth century shows that these three (along with other Jewish groups, important per se but smaller in size and influence) straddled a cultural map that crossed political borders and preserved identifying markers—linguistic, sociological, and ethnographic—formed centuries earlier. The boundaries between these Jewish ethnic communities reflected a geopolitical constellation that had long since disappeared. For example, the separate Yiddish dialects and the different cooking and baking customs of the Ukrainian Jews and their "Litvak" (Lithuanian) brethren, which persist to this day, represented the ancient border between the Kingdom of Poland and the Great Duchy of Lithuania—a political boundary that was erased in the second half of the sixteenth century! Similarly, until a few generations ago, one could find an "Aragon *kahal*" and a "Castile *kahal*" in the cities of the Ottoman Empire (and of Palestine), vestiges of a geopolitical division that had been obliterated before the Jews of Spain and Portugal had been forced to leave.

In the subsequent two hundred years, the population of these three diasporas underwent significant changes in magnitude; they were also displaced, replanted in faraway lands, and exposed to new regimes. They experienced cultural change at different paces due to differences in their exposure to the influences of modernity. One thing is clear, however: the map of premodern Jewish cultures did not surrender to changing geopolitical reality until the modern era. The Jews' cultural geography continued to cross national and imperial borders, to link communities beyond political frontiers, and to preserve administrative divisions of bygone empires.

At a certain juncture, the time of which varied from place to place and from empire to empire, an unprecedented change took place in the history of the Jews' relations with the political systems to which they were subject: the state began to meddle in the internal cultural life of the Jewish corporative entity (the *kahal*). The coalescence of centralized absolutist states and the advent of the ideas of the European Enlightenment—two political-cultural phenomena that spread steadily across Europe from France in the west to Germany and Austria and as far as Imperial Russia in the east— formed the motor of change and led ultimately to the creation of a totally new cultural reality. In the second half of the nineteenth century, the bulk

---

10. I use this word with a bit of discomfort and only because it has become common coinage; one might replace it with the term "Jews from Islamic countries" or "Judeo-Arabic culture."

of the three Jewish diasporas lived within the confines of four great empires: Imperial Germany, Austria-Hungary, Imperial Russia, and the Ottoman Empire.[11] The Jews were gradually exposed, at varying levels of intensity, to the intervention of the imperial regime (or of imperial and colonial agents of other European powers such as Britain, France, and Italy) in their community administration, education systems, and means of communication.

The *kehillah* (or *kahal*), which until then had enjoyed corporate autonomy under law and the protection of the various state authorities, steadily lost its ability to preserve the Jewish cultures that European thinkers dismissed as unworthy of preservation and in need of reformation. From the second half of the eighteenth century to the beginning of the twentieth century, the Ashkenazi diaspora, from Alsace in the west to Lithuania in the east, came under the growing influence of imperial cultures, starting with the French, moving on to other cultures nurtured by Austria and Prussia, and ending with the Tsarist authorities' Russification policy. The Sephardi and Oriental diasporas were exposed to concurrent processes as French, British, and Italian colonialism made inroads in North Africa and the Middle East. Geopolitical circumstances determined the pace of acculturation from one community to the next.

The French example is a good case in point: Ashkenazi Jews from northeastern France and North African Jews entered the French Empire's cultural sphere of influence at the beginning of the modern period. In Algeria, Tunisia, and Morocco, Jews encountered the colonial regime introduced by the imperial culture, borne by emigrés from France who had settled in a colony (mainly in Algeria), or by Jewish philanthropic organizations that disseminated the imperial culture (the Alliance israélite universelle). In Alsace, the district that France had annexed in the late seventeenth century, the Republican regime wished to integrate the Yiddish-speaking Ashkenazi Jews into the state culture, while abolishing the autonomy of the *kehillah*. In Ottoman communities outside the French-ruled areas, the French imperial culture was disseminated by a network of Alliance schools that were administered from headquarters in Paris.[12]

Thus, the influence of European culture spread across the Jewish diaspora following two parallel paths. One was the imperial path, which originated from the second half of the eighteenth century onward in the

---

11. These empires were dissolved in 1918. For the sake of clarity, the ensuing uses of "Austria" refers to the eastern provinces of the Habsburg Empire before 1918, including Galicia (Austrian Poland), unless otherwise noted.

12. For a critical study of the Alliance educational network in the Ottoman Empire, see Aron Rodrigue, *French Jews, Turkish Jews: The Alliance Israélite Universelle and the Politics of Jewish Schooling in Turkey, 1860–1925,* Modern Jewish Experience (Bloomington: Indiana University Press, 1990).

multinational empires where most of world Jewry lived: Imperial Russia, Austria (or, from 1867 onward, the Austro-Hungarian Empire); and the second was the colonial path, through which European cultures reached almost all Jewish communities in the Mediterranean basin. The Jews' exposure to European cultural influence and their integration into modernization processes were not necessarily related to their migration to Palestine.

As we have seen, the Jewish collective in Palestine—the Old Yishuv— had been for centuries an immigrant society composed of groups of Jews who had come from disparate diasporas and preserved, each in its own way, their connection with their communities of origin. A slow and multigenerational process of migration that, accelerated during the nineteenth century, delivered new strata of immigrants, one after another—a process that preceded the national Aliyot of the late nineteenth and twentieth centuries. However, these immigrant groups that arrived, wave after wave, from the early nineteenth century on came not from a static cultural situation but from constantly changing cultural environments. They were squeezed between the desire to preserve their premodern culture and the pressure (and allure) exerted by the imperial culture that was initially imposed under duress but ultimately won over large segments of the Jewish population.

More than this, however, the Jews' identification with the imperial regime, and the culture that it imposed on the periphery, led to increasing friction with members of neighboring ethnic groups that wished to maintain their own cultural singularity. Quite paradoxically, the Jewish immigrants who had abandoned the empire in favor of the ancient Land of the Patriarchs brought with them a Russian or German imperial version of Western culture.

In pre-1881 Palestine, one could find nuclei of immigrant groups that had settled there more than a century earlier and had remained there without interruption. Various researchers have estimated the population of the pre-Zionist Yishuv on the eve of the First Aliyah at around 24,000, the size of one medium-sized community in the Pale of Settlement of Imperial Russia.[13] Still, despite its diminutive size, the Yishuv was a microcosm of the social and cultural processes that were sweeping the entire diaspora. It accommodated some Jews who continued to nurture one of the premodern Jewish cultures that were endangered in the multinational empires of central and eastern Europe. There were also cultural agents who had reached the Middle East from each of these empires and wished

---

13. The demography of Palestine in the late-Ottoman period has been for decades an academic minefield. I rely here on what I consider a least politically biased research: Alexander Scholch, "The Demographic Development of Palestine, 1850–1882," *International Journal of Middle East Studies* 17.4 (1985): 485–505.

to fit the Jews of Palestine into the acculturation processes of the places they had left. Furthermore, even at that early time, there were to be found some who desired to create a Jewish culture on the shores of the Mediterranean that, although new, would be Western in complexion. It was to be under the patronage of the empires and would participate in the integration of the metropolitan empire's Jewish subjects.

For its part, the Ottoman regime in Palestine hardly meddled at all in its ethnic subjects' cultural lives. Its representatives showed no interest in imposing the state culture on them, let alone doing what the imperial authorities in central and eastern Europe had done—establishing special school systems to hasten the cultural integration of the Jewish subjects into the empire.

Under the British Mandate (1920–1948), too, the government did not interfere in the cultural lives of Palestine's diverse communities. Unlike the colonial French, the British did not pursue a *mission civilisatrice.* Its officials neither took official action to educate the indigenous populations nor attempted to steer the cultural development of the inhabitants—Jewish or Arab—toward cultural Englishness. Furthermore, Palestine had been entrusted to Britain as a mandate and not taken as a colony. Consequently, the Mandate authorities in Palestine were perceived as temporary overseers of the country whose job was to ready it for political independence.[14]

The Ottoman and British authorities' lack of interest in the natives' cultures may explain how the various imported cultures in Palestine survived on parallel paths without being overtaken by a single dominant culture or assimilating into each other. In the cultural void that the authorities left, certain groups attempted to seize the prerogative. In the New Yishuv, the activity of the national movement and the cultural endeavors of numerous political groups and ideological organizations assumed many of the functions of a central government. The abundant variety and broad ideological diversity of these groups and organizations gave rise to overlapping subcultures that shaped what one may call a sectorial Hebrew culture—a sociocultural phenomenon that typified Israel in its early years.

The Balkan countries—Greece, Serbia, and Bulgaria—were the home of much of the Sephardi diaspora, and it was not coincidental that the first awakenings of modern Jewish nationalism there bore a strong resemblance to the awakening of the Ḥibat Tsiyon movement in eastern Europe in the 1880s. Nor is it a coincidence that a significant number of the immigrants who arrived in Palestine with the First Aliyah were from the northeastern segment of the new Romanian state, which had just wrested its

---

14. See Halperin, *Babel in Zion,* 16: "Jews were neither the ruling power nor the powerless natives. Rather, they were a small but elite nationalist group constituting itself under European Imperial rule and exercising a notable degree of leverage over the ruling power."

dependence from the Ottoman Empire in 1878. There was a historical connection between the disintegration of the empires—the spinning-off of nation states—and the stirring of the new Jewish national movement. Witnessing the disintegration around them, the Jews ceased to consider themselves an autonomous corporative entity under government protection but rather viewed themselves as an ethnic group with a culture of its own. The pressure on them no longer emanated from an empire that demanded their cultural integration (insofar as such pressure had existed before); instead, it originated in a nation-state where the political regime and the dominant culture were one and the same, that is, where the culture of *one* of the neighboring ethnic groups in the multiethnic empire had become the *dominant* culture.

The pressure applied by a national culture in a nation-state exceeds that of the imperial regime by far. An imperial culture is by nature universalistic, without inner borders, and nonethnic, leaving room for some ethnic variation. The *national* culture of a nation-state, in contrast, is loath to compromise with other ethnic groups that remain in the territory that it controls. The Jews were thus inherently predisposed to identify with imperial authorities—unless the latter breached religious or cultural limits in ways that the traditional society could not accept. Once adapted to an imperial culture or to a culture of one of the colonial empires, the Jews responded to the new changes in one of three ways: by clinging to the imperial culture, by making a cultural-linguistic adjustment to the new situation, or by developing their own ethnic identity and pursuing a Jewish cultural-national renaissance project. The upshot of this was that the new Hebrew culture that immigrants from the toppled empires sought to create in Palestine was continually torn between the universalistic imperial tradition and the single-nation cultural tradition that developed in eastern Europe and the Balkans.

As modernization in the diasporas gathered strength, however, relations among immigrants from the diasporas in Palestine, that had previously shown no propensity to intermingle and had allowed no modern ideology—national or other—to affect the nature of their relations with the other groups, began to change too. Whether it was still an element of a premodern culture (e.g., that of the Old Yishuv communities) or an imperial culture that the immigrants had acquired in their countries of origin, it represented the intense encounter with the challenges of modernity. Immigrants from Lithuania who lived in Jerusalem and Safed in 1840–1880 had experienced government-sponsored Enlightenment—Imperial Russia's massive intervention project—and they feared the influence of religious reform, promulgated by Jewish philanthropists from Austria. The old woman in Nahalal, who waxed nostalgic in the 1940s about how lovers used to discuss Russian belles lettres, recalled this youthful experience from the era when the Jewish bourgeoisie of the Pale of Settlement, on the western fringes of Imperial Russia, adopted these and other affectations of the imperial culture. The *yekke* (German Jew) who lived in the Rehavia neighborhood of Jerusalem in the late Mandate period, recited German poetry and had brought opulent editions of "The Complete Writings of..." from his abandoned home in Germany—complemented by porcelain coffee service—was following the custom of the pre-World War I liberal bourgeoisie of the German *Reich*.

The cultural baggage that the immigrants and migrants carried in their minds, hearts, and crates of books was no longer "traditional" in the pre-eighteenth-century sense. All of them—the Hasid from Ukraine, the Talmudic scholar from Lithuania, the revolutionary *halutsa* (Zionist pioneer women) from eastern Europe, and the *yekke* professor of the Hebrew University—had already undergone a lengthy and complex cultural process that included contacts with surrounding cultures, the internalization of their influences, acculturation, self-defense against attempts at reeducation, and adjustment to new realities. The Jews' acculturation was thus imported to Palestine from several imperial environments and in various degrees of intensity. In certain cases, the cultural process that the immigrant underwent was so intense as to induce him or her to drop the traditional vernacular and take up an imperial language at a stroke. In other cases, it was a gradual process with minor effects that were much harder to distinguish.

One cannot find a better example of such a cultural cornucopia than the interimperial encounter of cultures that occurred during the First Aliyah, the neonatal period of the national settlement project. Just consider Jewish life in Palestine in 1885. Yiddish-speaking settlers from the seam between the Ottoman Empire and Imperial Russia lived in the colonies of Rosh Pina and Zikhron Ya'akov. In Yesod Hama'ala pious Hasidim from Russian Poland mingled with North African Jews from Safed, while Gedera was settled by radical immigrants (those of the Bilu movement) brimming with influences of Russian radical political thought. They were all supervised by administrators in the service of Baron Edmond de Rothschild (1845–1934) of Paris, who ran the affairs of the new villages (which were one to three years old at the time!). Those agents of French imperial culture were Jews from North Africa, Alsace, and Imperial Russia—all teachers and/or alumni of the French Alliance school system. The *Kollel Ungarn*, an ultra-Orthodox organization in Jerusalem was closely connected with the village of Petaḥ Tiqva under the patronage of the Austro-Hungarian Empire, while a consular agent of the British Empire, a North African Jew, helped to buy lands for settlers from areas that Russia had captured from the Ottomans. It goes on and on....

Many of these cultural agents came from distant peripheries of their respective empires—places very far from the metropolis both geographically and culturally. On the whole, those who came to Palestine, at least until the end of World War I, from the multiethnic empires had not fought on the front lines in the wars of acculturation. It should also be noted that the distance from the metropolis, social marginality, and rich variety of imperial cultures that Palestine offered did much to fuel spontaneous processes that often pulled in directions opposite to those advocated by the agents of the recommended culture.[15]

At least culturally, the new Zionist activity in Palestine unified two trends that belonged to the broad imperial context of Jewish nationalism. The first of these was the Zionists' work to preserve Jewish ethnic identity in the multinational empires. In Imperial Russia, as in the Austro-Hungarian Empire, the Zionists' conduct before World War I fit into the efforts of all diasporic parties, including the socialist anti-Zionist Bund, to create a national bloc in the imperial parliament. The Zionist movement played an active role in parliamentary life in both empires; its platform not only preached mass emigration to Palestine but also included quite a few planks relating to the attainment of national and cultural autonomy in exile. In the resolutions of the Helsingfors (Helsinki) conference (1906), the Russian Zionists stated explicitly that they would cooperate with all Jewish parties in the pursuit of autonomous cultural rights for the Jews of Imperial Russia. The Zionists on the other side of the Austro-Hungarian frontier adopted similar positions.[16]

This trend—which one may call Zionist autonomism—influenced cultural activity at home but did something more: some Zionists considered seeking autonomy for the steadily evolving New Yishuv in Palestine and fitting it into the framework of a multinational Ottoman Empire. This was because the Jews of the Ottoman Empire were contending with a similar but not identical problem. That is, members of the Sephardi diaspora in the Balkan countries and the Mediterranean basin underwent processes that were not essentially different from those experienced by the Jews of eastern Europe.[17]

From this standpoint, Zionism before World War I was a manifestation of intraimperial ethnic nationalism. Conceived as a response to the problem posed by the multitude of ethnic groups in the empires of central and eastern Europe, it sought to cultivate a new kind of national culture, nationally distinct but at the same time part of the imperial cultural mosaic.

Yet, while the Zionists, along with other Jewish national movements, acted to preserve ethnic identity within the imperial framework, they also

---

15. The encounter with the Bedouins in Palestine, for example, made radical Russian pioneers, members of the Second Aliyah, opt for integration with the local communities.

16. "All-Russian Zionist Conference: The Helsingfors Program," in Paul Mendes-Flohr and Jehuda Reinharz, *The Jew in the Modern World: A Documentary History* (New York: Oxford University Press, 1980), 343–44.

17. Israel Bartal, "Jewish 'Autonomism' of the Second Aliyah" [Hebrew], in *The Land of Israel in 20th Century Jewish Thought*, ed. Aviezer Ravitzky (Jerusalem: Ben Zvi Institute, 2004), 272–90.

cultivated a vision of a Jewish version of the nation-state. In such a state, the development of the regime (i.e., the political and administrative apparatus), the nexus of nation and territory, and the restructuring of a national culture would form part of a single process. Rather paradoxically, the progenitors of the Palestinian Zionist version of the national culture were trying to do the very thing that had put a spoke in their wheel in eastern Europe and crowded them out of the new nation states, those postimperial political entities that grew out of the ruins of Tsarist Russia, Austria-Hungary, and the Ottoman constellation.

This cultural tendency, strongly radicalized by the agents of the nascent Hebrew culture in Palestine, acted to stamp out premodern cultural legacies while selectively integrating some parts of them in a secular-national way. The goal was to nationalize the imperial cultures that the new immigrants had brought with them in the waves of national immigration, that is, to translate, rework, and adapt them to the new Hebrew national discourse. The resurrection of the Hebrew language as the language of the postimperial nation-state's culture is a case in point. Whereas imperial authorities had urged the Jews to abandon the vernaculars of their premodern corporative settings in favor of the imperial tongue (Russian, German, Hungarian, Polish, French), it became conventional wisdom in Palestine that not only the vernaculars but also the imperial languages spoken by most of the immigrants should be replaced by the revived national language. Eliezer Perlman (better known by his *nom de plume,* Ben-Yehuda), who came from a provincial town in western Imperial Russia, was the cultural agent who elaborated the argument that one nation ought to have one standard language, a national language used in all realms of life and spoken by everyone.

The subject of the postimperial Hebrew nation-state was to be the new Jew, who would cleanse his cultural identity of the premodern Yiddish and imperial Russian languages, not to mention their rich cultures, in favor of an ancient Hebrew, dredged up from the depths of history and enriched with selected locutions from Arabic, the country's vernacular. These are exactly the four cultural strata that surfaced in the two ostensibly simple vignettes that circulated among the Palmachniks with which we started this chapter!

Eliezer Ben-Yehuda, like intellectuals in other national movements, internalized the idea of linguistic unity as a centerpiece of national identity—a substitute for a changing or disappearing religious identity.[18]

---

18. "The Jewish religion will, no doubt, be able to endure, even in alien lands; it will adjust its form to the spirit of the place and the age, and its destiny will parallel that of all religions. But the nation? The nation cannot live except on its own soil; only on this soil can it revive and bear magnificent fruit, as in days of old!" (Eliezer Ben-Yehuda, "A Letter" [1880], in *The Zionist Idea: A Historical Analysis and Reader,* ed. Arthur Herzberg [New York: Atheneum, 1984], 160–65, here 165).

Along with this, of course, went a territory shared by a solid majority of members of the national group. This idea, which wielded no small influence on the cultural policies of parties and groups under the British Mandate, resulted in the quite brutal exclusion of entire cultural sectors from the new national discourse. Nevertheless—as the stories in *Yalqut ha-kezavim* show—the bearers of those diverse cultures just carried on. Their spontaneous influence on the new Israeli culture still awaits study and research.

The multinational empires—arenas of rapid modernization that inundated Jewish communities on the eastern and southern fringes of Europe—were the wombs from which sprang Hebrew culture in Palestine. The exposure of most of world Jewry to Western influences took place not via direct contact with the West but rather through the filter of one empire or another, its administrators from within and its agents from without. The premodern Jewish cultures of the early modern period, diluted by the cultural influence of the multinational empires, reached Palestine with the waves of new immigrants in the late nineteenth and early twentieth centuries. Here they encountered a powerful national ideology whose bearers sought to establish a nexus of politics and culture—exactly as had happened in the nation-states that were torn from the multinational empires in the Balkans, central Europe, or eastern Europe. The painful encounter between the imperial legacy and the vision of a Hebrew national culture—a vision also born and shaped in the dying days of the multinational empires—generated tensions, imposed changes, and fomented counterreactions. Various cultural traditions, which were tolerated in Imperial Russia, the Austro-Hungarian Empire, or the Ottoman Empire but rejected in the Israeli incarnation of the modern nation-state, demanded, and still demand, a place for themselves in Israeli society. They have become part of the present-day Israeli cultural mosaic either by accepting the supremacy of the national discourse or by demonstratively seceding from it.

Fiery clashes on cultural issues, often political in nature, continue to take place in contemporary Israel. Many segments of the ultra-Orthodox community participate, as do intellectuals and politicians who claim to represent various currents of "Oriental culture," and officials of government offices, who seek to shape Israeli culture according to one ideological formula or another. A close and critical examination of the contents, the discourse, and the tactics employed reveals that the current disputes on issues such as the attitude of rabbis to the army, the status of the Hebrew language, the music played on Israeli radio stations, or what is studied in the public schools, have their roots in the pre-1914 imperial era. Today's conflicts can thus be seen simply as further chapters in the cultural and historical story that began with the transition of the Jews from members of various premodern ethnoreligious corporations to groups of subjects in multinational empires.

4

Upstairs, Downstairs:
Yiddish and *Ivrit* in Tel Aviv

In his book *Tseḥok me-Erets Yisrael* (Laughter from the Land of Israel), a collection of humoristic articles about Tel Aviv culled from the Hebrew press of the 1930s and 1940s, the bilingual American-Jewish writer Daniel Persky (1887–1962) describes an old Tel Aviv type. The man regularly worshiped at the "Great" Synagogue (Hebrew: *beit ha-knesset ha-gadol*) in the so-called first Hebrew city (Hebrew: *ha-ir ha-ivrit ha-rishonah*):

> Three times a day he would pray in the "downstairs *minyan*" in the cellar of the Great Synagogue on Allenby Street. This *paloosh* [*polish* in Yiddish—synagogue entrance foyer—Ed.] was folksy and accessible to the general public. It had a special merit: rabbinical storytellers and exegetes were allowed to lecture there in Yiddish, and prayer services there were conducted in the Ashkenazi accent—two cardinal sins in the magnificent Great Synagogue proper, where everything was as *Ivrit* as could be. Truth to tell, the people who ran the place banned these two "crimes" in the *paloosh*, too, but they hardly ever went downstairs to see what was going on. Therefore, the shackles were loosened there.[1]

Persky goes on to describe the reality of this everyman's place of worship that he saw when he chanced to be there during the interval between the afternoon and evening services:

> Noticing a crowd packing into the downstairs *paloosh*, I went in and there he was, a preacher delivering a sermon in sweet Yiddish and in an old-time singsong tone; and there was the crowd, *kvelling* with satisfaction.[2]

---

1. Daniel Persky, *Tseḥok me-Erets Yisrael* (New York: Futuro Press, 1951), 264. Persky was a prolific Hebrew journalist and editor who emigrated from the Russian Empire to the United States in 1906. Persky was a sworn Hebraist, whose visiting card bore the legend "I am a slave of Hebrew forever." His numerous articles were published both in Israeli and North American Jewish newspapers.

2. Ibid.

This Tel Aviv story from the early 1930s (Persky lived there 1930–1933), provides a unique perspective on the culture that took shape in what was once called "the first Hebrew city."

As Persky would have it, two cultures coexisted in young Tel Aviv at that time. Upstairs, at street level and on the upper floors, Hebrew culture was dominant—the culture dictated by cultural agents, New Yishuv politicians, and newspapermen. Downstairs, in the basement—under the surface—a venerable and authentic grassroots culture flourished, reaching straight from the *shtetlekh* of eastern Europe to Allenby Street in the Middle East. The former was a new culture, official and detached from its folk roots; the latter, a culture drawn from direct contact with simple folk, artisans, and shopkeepers and umbilically connected to the world of *galut,* the Jewish exile. Ostensibly, the former held sway and even dictated limits to the one downstairs; still, the latter, although theoretically under the other's heel, enjoyed *de facto* freedom.

The upstairs Hebrew culture was an artificial creation of an elite in thrall to a dream; the Yiddish culture of the cellar was natural and authentic, flowing spontaneously and directly from the living bond between the people themselves and their premodern heritage from eastern Europe. Furthermore, old and deeply rooted customs flourished downstairs: it was a traditional folk performance that took place, a juicy sermon in Yiddish in a specifically religious context. Upstairs, in contrast, the agents of the new Hebrew culture consigned continuity and rootedness to extinction. Upstairs—young Hebrew speakers, their cultural roots planted in the shifting sands of Tel Aviv. Downstairs—old men preserving a centuries-old culture with roots firmly planted in deep subterranean strata.

A deeper look at the story reveals further aspects of culture in the first Hebrew city. Daniel Persky, a scholar well versed in the Jewish culture of eastern Europe, was at home with what was taking place on both floors of Tel Aviv's Great Synagogue. In conceptual terms, he identified with the linguistic and cultural renewal that the Zionist enterprise in Palestine had awakened and enthusiastically monitored the growth of the new *ivri'yut* (Hebrewism) in the city. Deep down, however, he felt a bond with the culture of the synagogue's cellar. It lured him in; it was that for which he *kvelled* (burst with pride).

What is more, Persky had good reason to set his portrayal of the tension between the programmatic Hebrew culture and the exilic culture, crowded out and relegated to the netherworld of the cellar, specifically in the Great Synagogue of Tel Aviv. It was there, one might say, that the seam between the two cultures ran. The preferential Hebrew culture and the spurned Ashkenazi culture touched through the narrow slab that separated the two floors of the building. Here, in effect, a Land-of-Israel chapter in the secularization of Jewish society unfolded—in the sense not of the disappearance of religion from life but of its transformation and enlistment into the service of "national" needs to become part of a national culture manufactured and shaped by politicians and officials.

In the Great Synagogue, the role of religion in the public life of the first Hebrew city was diminished. It was cut off from the folk culture of the diaspora and connected to the secular Zionist public sphere by means of a sterile, choral temple architecturally reminiscent of the sort that was common in the great cities of pre–World War II central and eastern Europe. As we have seen, a cement slab separated the Hebrew story of the new Tel Aviv temple from the basement, where Yiddish reigned but, to be honest, the upper floor was standing on the shoulders of the lower.

That upper culture crowded out the lower one. It shoved it into the cellar and tried to imprison it there. The downstairs culture, however, did not submit. It broke out and made its way upstairs, engaging the popular spirit and showing the people up top just how shallow and weak their thinking was. To put it another way, the culture of the cellar was historically and culturally authentic and so formed a persistent threat and irksome challenge to the new official culture of Tel Aviv.

A. A Middle Eastern Strain of Modernism

Thus it was that an eagle-eyed journalist in the first Hebrew city noticed on the Allenby Street of the early twentieth century a clash of cultures that had begun in the Jewish communities of Europe in the latter decades of the eighteenth century. It was no less than the standoff between Western-oriented modernism, which aspired to create a new Jewish culture for the Jews, and the masses of Ashkenazi Jews, who, some more and some less, wanted to preserve their cultural heritage. The presence of thousands of immigrants from Russia and Poland had always challenged the threatening cultural colonialism that infiltrated the great cities of western Europe, and their resistance had now spread to Hebrew Tel Aviv.

Tel Aviv's *ivri'yut*, though ostensibly nativist, proved to be yet another, wholly new, strain of Jewish modernism whose goal was to replace Yiddish, the traditional vernacular of the Jewish masses in the Ashkenazi diaspora. This time it was not with High German, Imperial Russian, or the Hungarian of Budapest but with an ancient Semitic tongue, the one taught in the schools of Palestine on the basis of the Hebrew Bible.

Few (if any) today remember that, for several generations in the modern era, the adjective "Hebrew" denoted something that contrasted with "Jewish." The only group that still remains aware of the novel anti-Jewish connotation of the word "Hebrew" is the ultra-Orthodox, customarily known in Israel as the *Haredim*. With their sensitive cultural antennae (which are quintessentially ahistorical), a Jew is someone whose pulse throbs with the totality of the postbiblical Jewish textual tradition, that is, the continuity of creative endeavor from the Mishnah down to the rabbis of the twentieth century.

In the *Haredi* world, Scripture exists as something that has been incorporated and assimilated into the Talmudic-Midrashic whole. The modern Hebrew language, the one reconstituted by the Maskilim and secularized by Zionist authors, poets, philosophers, and pioneers, is spiritually foreign to them. Many of them believe to this day, that *Ivrit* is just another vernacular, a language that has nothing in common with *loshon ha-qoydesh,* the holy tongue of the sources (in Ashkenazi pronunciation). The Hebrew Bible as a work of literature, the historical documentary basis of a modern nation, and a fortiori the key to the reconnection of a nation to its ancient land, is altogether alien for them.

It was on these grounds that an eminent ultra-Orthodox leader in Israel recently attacked the way history is taught in Israel's nonreligious public schools. After all, for the *Haredim,* Zionist-style historiography, which secularizes the ancient past and wants to replace the exilic "Jew" with the Israeli "Hebrew," is just one of many heretical manifestations of Jewish nationalism.[3]

"Hebrewism" (*ivri'yut*) as a challenge to Judaism appeared in the very first stages of the acculturation that the Jews underwent in their contact with the cultures of Europe, either within Europe itself or in the European colonies in the Mediterranean basin. The revulsion felt by non-Jews in modern Europe in face of the Jewish other and their disgust for the Jews' language, physical characteristics, attire, mores, and occupations made the word "Jew" (or *Juif, Jude, Zhid,* etc.) into a pejorative epithet. The reforms that the Maskilim demanded in order to remove the stigma of otherness were predicated on, among other things, the suppression of the term "Jew"' and its replacement with a respectable alternative. Thus, reformists, philo-Semites, and, above all, liberal-minded Jews, who were tired of coping with their coreligionists' negative traits, replaced the word "Jew" in almost every European language with a different term — Hebrew, *Yevrey,* but also Israelite, Izraelit, etc.[4]

So the Zionists who sought to reconstitute a Hebrew culture in the Land of the Patriarchs were not the first to exchange Jewishness for Hebrewness. In fact, the path they proposed seemed simpler than that of other innovation-minded Jewish movements. Their Hebrew enterprise was able

---

3. On the *Haredi* school curriculum of history as counterhistory responding to modernism, see Kimmy Kaplan, "The Formation of Israeli Haredi Collective Historical Memory: Textbooks for High Schools Students," in *Army, Memory and National Identity* [Hebrew], ed. Moshe Naor (Jerusalem: Magnes, 2007), 177–94 [Hebrew].

4. Note the biblical etymology and the positive Christian allusions of the preferred terms.

to claim a geographical-historical nexus of language, Scripture, and the nature of the land—an advantage that could be matched only with difficulty, if at all, in the streets of Odessa or the alleys of Warsaw. In fact, the new Hebrewness of Tel Aviv on the Mediterranean coast resembled the Germanness exhibited by quite a few Prussian Jews in the nineteenth century except for the fact that it had developed *ex nihilo* rather than flowing from accommodation to a political culture that had already crystallized elsewhere in the country.

The more Hebrew the new Tel Aviv culture was, the less Jewish it was. It derived its Hebrewness from the Jewish sources but did so by reading them in a very selective manner, filtering out old components to help promote the creation of a cultural system unprecedented in Jewish history.

B. Colorful Exterior, Shallow Interior

The ideologically driven attempt to create a new Hebrew culture in Palestine was therefore linked to the world of European modernity. The national culture presented as something new to the *tsabarim*, the girls and boys of the new native generation raised on the edges of the sand dunes north of Jaffa, was in fact merely a metamorphosis of something deeply rooted in Western soil. To make things even more complicated, the "West" of many champions of the new Hebrew culture was, in fact, an east European metamorphosis of something western that had reached late nineteenth-century Imperial Russia in Russian translation.

Tel Aviv itself was something like a sociocultural laboratory where intellectuals, writers, journalists, and party functionaries—nearly all from two empires on the eastern and southern fringes of Europe—concocted a variegated brew that would eventually be called a New Hebrew culture. They did this by blending Romantic nationalism of German and Polish manufacture; radical populism imported from Tsarist Russia; a pinch of the Haskalah legacy; a dose of *belles lettres*, theater, and painting of the Moscow, St. Petersburg, Odessa, or Warsaw persuasion; and a dash of nostalgia for a Jewish past that had never existed except in their imagination.

Nonetheless, nostalgia for the recent eastern European past was mixed with loathing and contempt. The first Hebrew city assembled a mélange of impassioned visionaries, inspired by the works of the Haskalah author Abraham Mapu and Herzl's Zionist utopia *Altneuland* (translated into Hebrew by Nahum Sokolow and published under the title *Tel Aviv*), with school principals, leaders of culture, actors and directors, composers of music, and organizers of public rituals and festivals who looked for their inspiration elsewhere. The new cultural patterns that this motley group fashioned in Tel Aviv more closely resembled those of Europe's great cities than the forms of diaspora Jewry's traditional cultures.

The agents of the new culture, although well aware of the quintessentially European complexion of the neonatal Hebrew culture, presented their enterprise as a shining model of national endeavor, derived directly from ancient and pure sources. And indeed, the national intellectuals did call on ancient sources for their new cultural project. They returned to the Bible and the story of the Maccabees, searching for national uprisings, as well as expressions of physical resilience, heroism, and love of homeland. However, their choice of sources, the way they interpreted them, and the connections they established between the sources and ideas, symbols, and rituals were foreign to the traditional Jewish world.

This emerges in sharp relief when we study the sources by which the agents of the formative Hebrew culture documented the way they celebrated the Hanukkah and Purim festivals in Tel Aviv. Of these, it was Hanukkah, of all Jewish observances, that the new national movement subjected to the most revolutionary changes. At the very dawn of the *Ḥibat Tsiyon* (Love of Zion) movement in the early 1880s, Hanukkah was chosen as the time to celebrate the Jews' abandonment of passivity, physical weakness, and impotence vis-à-vis the mighty *goy* in favor of bellicose activism, resilience, and the ability to fight back. The Zionists went on to strip Hanukkah of its character as a religious festival observed mainly in the home and recast it as a public event of a political nature. They linked the festival to calisthenics, sports competitions, and rallies and transformed it into a holiday eminently suited to take on the characteristics of national rituals in other countries. Perhaps most tellingly, Zionist practice exchanged the *al ha-nissim* ("For the Miracles") prayer, which thanked God for the miraculous deliverance of Hanukkah, for the song *"nes lo kara lanu"* ("No miracle happened to us"), in which the miraculous nature of the festival is flatly disavowed. Even the ritual of lighting candles on indoor windowsills morphed into a candlelight parade or a torch-lit race down the city streets.

Hebrew Tel Aviv was both symbolically and practically the appropriate setting for this new national Hanukkah ritual. Once uncoupled from Jaffa in the early 1920s, it had become a city with a preponderant Jewish majority. The self-rule that the Jewish municipality enjoyed there was pronouncedly national in nature and encouraged public rituals in public places. An account of the candlelight parade in early Tel Aviv, a procession of thousands of schoolchildren carrying Hanukkah candles down the city streets, illustrates the point. An observer, the Labor Zionist journalist Aharon Ze'ev Ben-Yishai (1902–1977), described the cheering mass procession as follows. This is not the Hanukkah of *galut* (exile), in which "there is darkness all around, terror all around … and voices … shouting at them from the Christians' vaulted church."[5] Instead, he insisted proudly, "Look at those little ones marching erect, heads straight and necks extended, in this fresh spring-like autumn air, the air of late Kislev in the Hebrew city. This is a procession of free people!"[6]

However, as the study of national movements and the history of public rituals in European cities in the modern era demonstrates, the event described here is not a venerable and venerated Jewish ceremony but a totally new secular one.[7] It was a ritual overflowing with the worship of youth and admiration for the physical strength that Jewish society had just recently acquired. Wholly a rebellion against the old ways of doing things and a rejection of exilic weakness, Hanukkah in the Hebrew Tel Aviv of the 1930s was also the demonstrative adoption of "gentile ways" (Hebrew: *darkhei hagoyim*). Though more than a little pathos-ridden, this heroic phase of the old-new national movement overturned the traditional meaning of an ancient festival and imported the parades and public displays of the plazas of central European cities to the Hebrew streets of the new national setting.

Purim in Hebrew Tel Aviv, in contrast, reveals the subversive and blatantly nonnational fundamentals of this movement. This festival, unlike Hanukkah, features several cultural elements that the shapers of the new Hebrew culture found hard to reconcile with standing tall on the soil of the homeland. The nexus of Purim and the first Hebrew city[8] deserves close examination because it reveals a number of the undercurrents that flowed from the traditional world to the new culture that was ostensibly growing on its own on the shallow dunes of Tel Aviv, exactly as seen in the cellar of the Great Synagogue.

Purim was and remains the most non-Jewish festival in the Jewish calendar. It has blatantly pagan elements; it may be the only day on which anyone who feels like it may (at least by tacit consent) challenge the traditional order of things, including personal sobriety. Furthermore, it was on

---

5. Aharon Ze'ev Ben-Yishai, "taha'lukhat ha-nerot be-Tel-Aviv" (The Candle Procession in Tel Aviv), in *Sefer Ha-mo'adim* (Book of Festivals), vol. 5 (Tel Aviv, 1954), 5:254–55.

6. Ibid., 255.

7. For a discussion of similar cases of nationalist rituals in modern Europe, see Avner Ben-Amos and Eyal Ben-Ari, "Resonance and Reverberation: Ritual and Bureaucracy in the State Funerals of the French Third Republic," *Theory and Society* 24 (1995): 163–91; Ulf Hedetoft, "Nationalism as Civil Religion and Rituals of Belonging before and after the Global Turn," in *Holy Nations and Global Identities: Civil Religion, Nationalism, and Globalisation*, ed. Annika Hvithamar, Margit Warburg, and Brian Arly Jacobsen, International Studies in Religion and Society 10 (Leiden: Brill, 2009), 253–70.

8. Hizki Shoham, "A Huge National Assemblage: Tel Aviv as a Pilgrimage Site in Purim Celebrations (1920–1935)," *Journal of Israeli History* 28.1 (2009): 1–20.

Purim that Jews throughout the diaspora continued to pummel Haman and avenge themselves on their enemies (at least symbolically).

The two heroes of the Book of Esther, Mordechai and Hadassah (Esther), acted on behalf of their people using those methods of intercession (Hebrew: *shtadlanut*) that proud Zionists loved to besmirch, including winning concessions in the bedroom. Despite this, however, the new Hebrew culture of "Little Tel Aviv" (Hebrew: *tel aviv haktanah*) of the Mandatory era was drawn to this of all festivals and made it into a wild carnival of crude anti-Diasporic Hebrewism.

The scholar of Jewish folklore Yom-Tov Lewinsky (1899–1973) aptly put his finger on the points of intersection between the festival of licentiousness, drunkenness, and Haman bashing and the capital of the Israeli culture-in-formation. He christened Little Tel Aviv the *"ad-de-lo-yada* metropolis" (the "Until One Cannot Distinguish" City), referring to the injunction to get so drunk on Purim that one cannot distinguish between Haman and Mordechai—an expression that captured Purim's traditional loosening of inhibitions:

> It was for good reason that Tel Aviv, the youngest of the towns in Palestine, was chosen as the center for the renewed festival of Purim, the festival of religiously sanctioned frivolity, clowning, merriment, and "vengeance on the goyim." Indeed, there is nothing like this city, which constructs and deconstructs, deconstructs and constructs, sheds and acquires new skin overnight, a city that since its first day has been a multi-complexioned parade of types and languages and architectural forms and mannerisms and customs. A city that adopts non-style as its style and incomparable instability as its stability is well suited to being the metropolis of the jocular and the mocking, of derision and criticism, the city of clownishness.[9]

The writer—a passionate participant in the Jewish national movement's "cultural ingathering project" (Hebrew: *mif'al ha-kinus*)[10] and the editor of *Sefer ha-mo'adim* (Book of Festivals) inspired conceptually and practically by the teaching of Ḥayim Naḥman Bialik—obviously recognized how shallow the embryonic new culture in Tel Aviv really was. He keenly observed the eclecticism of the new Hebrewism, the tension between construction and deconstruction, and, above all, its instability. Hebrew Tel Aviv was for him a colorful shell that concealed a shallowness of thought

---

9. Yom-Tov Lewinsky, *"Ba-metropolin shel ha-ad-de-lo-yada,"* in *Sefer Ha-mo'adim* (Book of Festivals), vol. 6 (Tel Aviv, 1956), 286.

10. On *mif'al ha-kinus*, see Israel Bartal, "The Kinnus Project: *Wissenschaft des Judentums* and the Fashioning of a 'National Culture,'" in *Transmitting Jewish Traditions: Orality, Textuality and Cultural Diffusion*, ed. Yaakcov Elman and Israel Gershuni, Studies in Jewish Culture and Society (New Haven: Yale University Press, 2000), 310–23.

that was suppressing an immense cultural wealth, allowing only tiny drops of traditional culture to seep to the surface and blend into the thin, fragile coating.

C. Trying to Fill a Cultural Void

The new culture in Tel Aviv lacked one of the fundamental elements of any national movement that traced its origins to European Romanticism: authenticity. Its progenitors desperately needed a living, organic, and direct connection between their cultural product, the people, and the land (Hebrew: *am* and *arets*).

It was a tall order. They needed not only to populate the new city with a people created almost *ex nihilo* but also to connect the people in a satisfying way with the land, and to propose a vision of historical continuity that would cover the Zionists' demographic deficiencies, for in the late 1920s, fewer than two hundred thousand Jews lived in Palestine.[11] They also had to fill the void between the high culture that the new cultural engineers thought they had found in Hebrew literature, and the rejected, not to say reviled diaspora culture, which the population actually settling the country had brought with it.

The cultural ingathering of the Jewish people as conceived by several forerunners of Jewish national thought was supposed to inject elements of culture into the people that was settling in Zion. These included language, historical memory, and geographic knowledge, all of which seemed essential for the creation of something quite new that would represent at one and the same time a continuation of past traditions and a revolution against them.

The agents of the new national culture—the Hebrew teachers, the writers, the philosophers, the historians, and the scholars in Jewish Palestine—took it for granted that top-down cultural action could be integrated with natural, ground-up spontaneous development. The trouble was, however, that a spontaneous culture such as the one that flourished in the cellar of the Great Synagogue of Tel Aviv was just not inclined to listen to what the agents of the new culture had to say. Furthermore, spontaneous culture is, by its very nature, at odds with cultural planning of any kind and this one, in particular, had absolutely no connection with either the cultural standards inherited from the Haskalah or the products of modern secular nationalism.

The decidedly religious nature of the Jews' popular culture, which

---

11. E. Mills, Superintendent of Census, *Census of Palestine, Population of Villages, Towns and Administrative Areas* (Jerusalem, 1932), 1.

sometimes overpowered the national ideology that aimed to take the place of religious faith and observance of the commandments, posed a challenge and an internal threat to the doctrine of secular innovation. On the other hand, however, when the shapers of the new Hebrew culture wanted to give authenticity to their fledgling creation, they usually turned to the very folk culture that, though they had rebelled against it, continued to exist in their midst, and attempted to lift it out of its old contexts and to find in it sparks of a national culture. Such a decontextualization, which allowed the proponents of the new culture to translate an eastern European folk song from Yiddish into Hebrew, to flip an old folk saying on its head, and to fashion a Zionist folktale out of Diasporic materials, was part of an attempt to fill a great cultural void. Other cases in the history of modern nationalism tell us much about the national Romantics' need to fill their cultural voids with materials of the nation's past.

The projects of the new Hebrewism desperately needed a "folk culture" (Hebrew: *tarbut amamit*). Their version of this, however, proved to be in a constant struggle with other alternative folk cultures that different currents of Jewish nationalism dredged up. Among other things, the Tel Aviv innovators of Hebrewism made extensive use of the almost mythological "folk" of the eastern European Jewish masses on the eve of World War I. Their culture was, at that time, a source of inspiration for ethnographers and musicologists such as S. An-sky (1863–1920) and Joel Engel (1868–1927).[12] The latter actually came to little Tel Aviv a few years after World War I and joined the Hebrew revival movement.

Another folk culture that the Zionists claimed was the Jewish culture practiced among the communities of the Mediterranean basin, which seemed more authentic in the local context. Two additional sources of folk creativity figured significantly in fledgling Tel Aviv's quest for authenticity: one was the local culture of the country's Arab population, with which the Zionist settlers had been in contact since the 1880s; the other was the idealized culture of the non-Jewish rural lower classes in eastern Europe, which had left an impression on immigrants from those countries and would continue to serve as a cultural model in these formative years.

As the new Hebrew culture crystallized, each of these cultural alternatives found a place, thanks to the cultural agents who embraced them and due to spontaneous events and situations in the (New) Yishuv society. The different alternatives were accepted not *en bloc* but selectively and little by little: here an Arabic epithet, there an adage translated from Yiddish, somewhere a saying from Ladino, and so on. Each one was unhitched from its old traditional context and integrated into a totally new cultural matrix that was, in fact, intended to do away with all the old contexts.

---

12. This ethnomusicological project is discussed in chapter 7.

In Tel Aviv, therefore, the threatening absence of a coherent folk culture in the gestation of the new Hebrew culture was filled in by means of a complex interplay between the Zionist guiding hand and the stock of old cultures that the immigrants had brought with them or found when they arrived. The agents of the new culture, though they wanted to control the filling of the void, were terrified at the very idea that one of those authentic traditional cultures might rise up and challenge their hegemony.

Ideologically speaking, and for reasons rooted in Romantic national metaphors and the radical populism that permeated much of the new national movement, these cultural agents needed a folk culture. However, in the complex reality of an immigrant society that lacked a central government, and which was at the same time a society whose elites were rebelling against the traditional cultural legacy on which they had been raised, the question of how to relate to this sought-after folk culture could not be resolved with a single, consensual answer. So these spurned alternative cultures continued to exist in the first Hebrew city, flourishing alongside the official Hebrew culture even as it professed to despise them and portrayed them as threats to its primacy.

Thus, as the impassioned children who attended Zionist schools marched down the city streets each Hanukkah clutching blazing torches and mouthing the Hebrew lyrics of *"nes lo kara lanu,"* tailors, shoemakers, and cobblers lit their tiny candles on a sill in the basement of the Great Synagogue and thanked God for His miracles, singing *"al ha-nissim"* in a thick Ashkenazi accent. There were those who likened this to the coexistence of diverse rituals within a single culture, while others thought that they could discern two different and totally disconnected worlds celebrating two very different events. Many others heralded the torchbearers as harbingers of the national future and consigned those who thanked God for His miracles to a generation that was on its way out.

5

Revolution and Nostalgia:
The Changing Images of the *Shtetl*

Today, more than seventy years after the Holocaust, the concept of the eastern European *shtetl* hardly speaks to young Jewish Israelis under forty years of age—assuming that they do not live in one of the scores of *Haredi* communities that nestle in several Israeli towns. If at all, the *shtetl* is remembered as the place where the grandparents or great-grandparents of native Israelis of Ashkenazi extraction were born.

It was not like that in the Jewish society of the Yishuv in Mandatory Palestine and in Israel's first years. Back then, as the new Hebrew culture was taking shape, the memory of the *shtetl* played a highly influential role in shaping the image of the New Hebrew—that mythological hero, part-Jew and part-Cossack or Bedouin—who was supposed to supersede the eastern European exilic Jew.

Another sign of change can be seen in attitudes toward Christianity. Young Israelis today visit churches in Israel, Europe, and America and contemplate the statues of Jesus the Nazarene inquisitively. The sight of the tortured features of "that man" and the sound of church bells do not terrify them. The Jews of the eastern European *shtetl* and their offspring who reached Palestine in the first half of the twentieth century would have reacted differently to the sound of church bells and the spectacle of the Christian sculptures.

Years ago, I visited Częstochowa, Poland, the place where they discovered the Black Madonna, who is venerated throughout Catholic Poland. Every day thousands of pious Catholics throng to the great cathedral where the icon of the holy mother is on display. They push through the entrance to the church, pack its cavernous interior, and pray that Our Lady may save them. I visited Częstochowa in 1984 in the company of Israeli academics, nearly all of whom were born in Poland or Lithuania. Several members of the group entered the house of worship to observe the ceremony in which the Madonna was shown to the crowd of pious believers. Professor Shmuel Werses (1915–2010), the noted scholar of Hebrew and Yiddish literature, who had been born in Vilna and emigrated to

Palestine in the 1930s, refused to go in. Neither an Orthodox Jew nor, to the best of anyone's knowledge, the holder of extreme political views of any kind, he said simply, "I cannot go into their house of prayer."

Professor Israel Halpern (1910–1971), my mentor in eastern European Jewish studies, had been born in Białystok, Poland.[1] When I told him in 1970 that I had heard a Catholic Mass (accompanied by the music of Mozart and Schubert) at St. Stephen's Cathedral in Vienna, capital of Austria, he was puzzled. "You know," he said, "I've never seen what a Christian church looks like from the inside."

Shmuel Werses and Israel Halpern, by then two elderly scholars, brought with them the baggage of more than a millennium of Jewish–Christian estrangement when they moved from eastern Europe to Palestine as young men. Even in the fledgling Yishuv in the Middle East, this baggage did not disappear. For those who lived in the eastern European towns, the Christian world was right next door but was nevertheless considered hostile, foreign, and frightening. The dread and aversion that attached itself to anything with even a whiff of Christianity were carried to Palestine by the natives of the Lithuanian, Polish, and Ukrainian towns, whether their childhood experiences had been in the *shtetl* or on the Jewish streets of the big cities.

The scholar of Jewish folklore Dr. Yom Tov Lewinsky (1899–1973) described the following event in the memoir that he wrote about his attending *cheder*. The bells of the Catholic church in Zambrów, the *shtetl* where he was born, were ringing. A Christian funeral passed by as the bells sounded. The young children of the *cheder* listened to the clanging of the bells and, in Yiddish, chanted to the rhythm as the sound spread across the air of the *shtetl*: *Haynt aynes, morgn tseyn / yeder tog men zol dos zen* (Today one, tomorrow ten / if only we could see this every day).[2]

The writings left behind by Zionism's founding fathers, who moved to an "old-new" country to exchange the gloomy memory of the eastern European exile for the painful glare of the Middle Eastern sun, show that the *shtetl* experience continued to live on in the depths of these innovative immigrants' consciousnesses while the innovations of modernity— technology and the marvels of the capitalist marketplace—came together in various combinations to shatter the institutions of traditional Jewish society. Ironically, as radical nationalists, social reformers, and creators of the new culture, nearly all of them had rebelled against the world of their birth with the conscious desire to efface the *shtetl* consciousness of their

---

1. He specialized in the history of Jewish self-rule in pre-partition Poland and published the documents of the Council of Four Lands in 1945. See Israel Halpern and Israel Bartal, eds., *Pinkas va'ad araba aratsot*, 2nd ed., with an introduction by Shmuel Ettinger (Jerusalem: Mosad Bialik, 1990).

2. Unpublished manuscript, in my private collection.

origins. However, their hopes, inhibitions, and fears, though in different guises, traveled straight from the fields of Ukraine and the forests of Belarus to the Zionist farming villages of Judea and Galilee and forestalled any such revolution.

First, the image of the non-Jewish neighbor in the *shtetl*, that threatening eastern European *goy*, was transformed in the journey from the villages of Poland and Russia to Palestine and intersected with that of the local other. The Palestinian Arab, the settlers' new neighbor, assumed the place of the Slavic non-Jew in their consciousness. The scholar of Hebrew literature Gershon Shaked (1929–2006) published an article in 1979 on the metamorphoses of the figure of the non-Jewish stranger in modern Hebrew literature as it made its way from Poland and Russia to the Land of Israel:

> If so, when Hebrew literature reached Palestine, it brought the stereotype of a non-Jew (or stereotypes of non-Jews) with it like an infection. The socio-literary question was: will this literature transplant the stereotypes that it lifted from the fringes of the West into the heart of the East? Will the regnant attitude here, too, be one of a persecuted and defensive minority toward a persecuting and aggressive majority? Or of a "backward" and inferior minority toward a majority that ensnares it in the fetters of its culture? Will they try here, too, to perpetuate that stereotype (that exists in their minds) of a persecuted and enchanted thing, as violence and Eros—repulsion and attraction—serve in these confrontations with strangers in a horrific … multivalent admixture?[3]

In the imagination of the *Hashomer* fighters, too, the image of the Cossack warrior, the murderer who terrorizes the residents of the Ukrainian *shtetl*, converged with that of the armed Bedouin equestrian. The members of this quasi-military organization, striving to transform the trembling and impotent native of the *shtetl* into a cruel and fearless fighter, sought models of heroism and nobility in the image of the local warrior. The founders of *Hashomer*, socialist revolutionaries and passionate nationalists, brought with them the fantasy of establishing colonies of fighter-farmers from the Ukraine. These colonies would be similar to the Cossack settlements in the frontier areas of Imperial Russia—the opposite of the impotent, unmanly, Jewish *shtetl*. Similarly, they grafted the memory of Ukrainian peasants from the villages surrounding the *shtetl* onto the Palestinian fellahin (peasants) in the villages that surrounded the New Yishuv in Palestine.

These passionate young people who reached the old-new homeland in the first two decades of the twentieth century tended to perceive the

---

3. Gershon Shaked, "We Are All Chased, Only History Chases" [Hebrew], *Ma'ariv: Literature, Art, Criticism* (May 11, 1979), 45.

Jewish farming villages as *shtetlekh* and identified wholeheartedly with everyone whom the eastern European *shtetl* Jew feared. One of the pioneers in *Hashomer*, Yiga'el, recounted the shameful behavior of the farmers of Metullah, the northernmost Jewish settlement in Palestine, when they were attacked by Druze villagers, "a tribe that could send thousands of armed warriors into battle." In their cowardice, he said, the settlers of Metulla had behaved exactly like *shtetl* Jews, "a handful of members of a people persecuted and accustomed to giving in for thousands of years."[4]

As the yellowing, faded photos of the members of *Hashomer* in the 1900s show, they chose the non-Jewish side as the paragon of the new man whom they wanted to create in the old-new homeland. Bedecked in *kaffiyas*, the Jewish fighters rode noble steeds and dreamed of peasant-warrior colonies in the wilderness on the eastern side of the Jordan River. It was not the scholar, the merchant, or the *luftmentsh* (intellectual) from the *shtetlekh* in the Pale of Settlement in Imperial Russia whom they sought to implant in Palestine. Rather, they adopted the persona of the gentile from outside the *shtetl*, living close to nature—the "goy," free, strong, and healthy in body and mind. The members of *Hashomer* yearned to gallop on horseback across the open spaces surrounding their *moshava-shtetl*, free of their burdensome Jewishness and its shameful weakness, which had been transplanted, as it were, from the provinces of Imperial Russia to Judea, Samaria, and the Galilee.

The children and grandchildren of these men and women, the founders of the Yishuv, unlike the immigrants themselves, were no longer plugged directly into the *shtetl* experience. Rather paradoxically, they absorbed the spirit of the *shtetl* from the hostile Hebrew literature that their teachers, born in eastern Europe, crammed into them in their Zionist schools. Accounts of the degeneracy and ugliness of Jewish society in the Pale of Settlement by Mendele Moykher Sforim (1836–1917) garnished with the neo-Romantic tales of I. L. Peretz (1852–1915, translated into Hebrew by Shimshon Melzer in the 1950s), bequeathed to several generations of Israeli pupils a cast of characters that was very far from the real world of the *shtetl*. Stereotypes originating in critiques of European Jewish life by exponents of the Haskalah movement were thus planted in the soil of the embryonic Israeli culture. Books in Hebrew served young Palestine-born *sabras* in the Mandate era and Israel's first decades as a wide bridge across which knowledge and consciousness that had existed in eastern Europe (or had been memorialized *as if it had existed there*) were brought to the evolving entity in the faraway Middle East.

One example will be enough to illustrate how directly the tendrils of Europe stretched from the lands of the cold to the minds of the new Israelis.

---

4. Bartal, "Hanukkah Cossack Style," 149–50 n. 30.

The *Heroes and Martyrs* (Hebrew: *Giborim u-qedoshim*) volume of the *Ma'ayan Encyclopedia for Youth*, a series much beloved by Israeli adolescents in the 1950s, imparted the legacy of the pogroms, massacres, and defensiveness of seventeenth-century eastern European Jewry to young readers in the new homeland in the twentieth century. The encyclopedia had a clear didactic purpose. The preface "To the Young Reader," found in another volume of the encyclopedia titled *Giants of Jewry* (Hebrew: *Gedolim be-Yisrael*), explained it:

> The authors' intent in this book is to enrich your trove of knowledge, young reader, and to illuminate the way of life of the giants of the spirit among our people, the way they were raised, and the aspiration to inner truth, which they considered the purpose of their lives. Many of them often absorbed a full dose of ridicule and contempt as they took their first steps, stumbled, and experienced disillusionment. However, they overcame the insults and calumny that came their way, and their truth rose to the surface and became a living wellspring for their nation and a blessing for all of humankind.[5]

The historical sections of the encyclopedia, edited by Jewish intellectuals from Poland and Russia, were eastern European in spirit and in content and left an imprint on how their readers imagined the *shtetlekh* where their parents had been born. The Hebrew literature read by young people in Israel's first decades was of much the same character but was replete with derogatory images of the *shtetl* and its Jewish inhabitants—images shaped in the spirit of the Haskalah and radicalized under the influence of modern nationalism. These images did not fully correspond with the history of eastern Europe; nor did they square with the actual geography of the *shtetl*.

What historical account of the *shtetl* failed to make the voyage to Palestine in its entirety? For centuries, the Jews of the eastern European *shtetl* were but one component of an ethnoreligious organism that had its feet planted in the soil of the medieval Polish-Lithuanian Commonwealth. They were a pronouncedly urban element, religiously distinct, of a unique legal status, and culturally different and separate from the other classes in their society. The *shtetl* (as well as urban neighborhoods in several large cities in the Commonwealth) evolved in a slow process, centuries long, of Jewish migration and settlement in Europe's largest kingdom.[6]

The Jews had imported their singular Ashkenazi culture to eastern

5. "To the Young Reader," in *Giants of Jewry*, vol. 9 of *Ma'ayan Encyclopedia for Youth* (Tel Aviv, 1956), unpaginated.

6. Israel Bartal, "The Establishment of East European Jewry," in *The Early Modern Period (1500–1815)*, vol. 7 of *The Cambridge History of Judaism*, ed. Jonathan Karp and Adam Sutcliffe (Cambridge: Cambridge University Press, 2018), 226–56.

Europe from the towns of medieval Germany. Germany was also the source of the patterns of relations between the Jews and the Christian population of eastern Europe. In the Commonwealth, the Jewish migrants encountered the Catholic Church (in its Polish version), which their forefathers already knew well in their countries of origin. In addition, in the eastern reaches of the Commonwealth, they also encountered Greek Orthodox Christianity, the confession of the other Slavs in that vast empire. Thus, they had to contend with two versions of Christian enmity: Catholic and Orthodox.

Orthodoxy preserved the Byzantine legacy, augmented over the centuries by theological debates in the eastern Slavic domain between Christian and Jewish savants. The mass killing that swept Ukraine in 1648–1649 (and was etched into the collective memory of the eastern European Jewish communities as the "slaughter of *taḥ-tat*," the years of the events in the Jewish calendar) were perpetrated by Orthodox Christians. By contrast, the blood libels in Poland, rather common occurrences in the *shtetlekh* from the late seventeenth century on, took place in a decidedly Catholic context.[7]

The segregation of the Jews' religious world from that of the regnant confessions in eastern Europe perpetuated various traditions rooted in the medieval German Jewish–Christian standoff. It was a standoff rife with tension, in which memories of slaughter and forced conversion mingled with hopes for revenge and expectations of redemption. Indeed, an Ashkenazi-style craving for divine revenge[8] can be seen to have made its way from the communities of Germany to eastern Europe. Even when the ideas of the European Enlightenment dulled the influence of the memory of this ancient standoff in Berlin and Frankfurt, it persisted in the *shtetlekh* of the Pale of Settlement in Imperial Russia. In Poland and Russia, the confrontation endured until the modern era, alive in the hearts and prevalent on the tongues of millions of Jews.

A conspicuous example of the vitality of those old memories from Medieval Ashkenaz may be seen in the persistence of blood libels in Poland. In the eighteenth century, by which time the idea of accusing Jews of murdering Christian children for religious ritual purposes had almost vanished in western and central Europe, blood libels were common in

---

7. "In Poland, as in the West, most of the ritual murder literature was produced by the Roman Catholic clergy.... In Poland, some of the eighteenth-century cases were orchestrated by the highest echelons of the clergy, and the proponents of the accusation produced imposing, if terrifying, literature. Local clergy at times openly rejected the papal pronouncements that denied the truth of the blood libel." From Paweł Maciejko, *The Mixed Multitude: Jacob Frank and the Frankist Movement, 1755–1816,* Jewish Culture and Contexts (Philadelphia: University of Pennsylvania Press, 2011), 96–97.

8. Israel Yuval, "Vengeance and Damnation, Blood and Defamation: From Jewish Martyrdom to Blood Libel Accusation" [Hebrew], *Zion* 58 (1993): 33–90.

Poland. With the approach of Passover each year, the *shtetl* was seized anew with dread: what if a dead Christian child were found in the Jewish neighborhood? It was a mystical thing, beyond the bounds of logic. Neither the new perspectives of the Haskalah nor the attainments of modern science dislodged the fears that had solidified on both sides.

The reciprocal xenophobia was perpetuated in the folklore and folk beliefs of eastern Europe. Polish peasants and townspeople truly believed that Jews used Christian blood in the baking of *matzah*. The Jew dwelt in their midst, ostensibly a human being just like them, but, in the belief of many, with something of the demon in him. The *shtetl* Jews, in turn, were convinced that the masses of *goyim* (non-Jews) surrounding their *shtetl* thirsted for their blood and coveted their property. To this very day, although Poland hardly has a rural Jewish population, the supernatural image of the Jew who has an ongoing relationship with Satan lives on in the popular culture. In some villages, one can still find wood and cloth dolls of a traditionally dressed Jew who carries a devil with a rooster's legs on his back.[9]

The literary map of the *shtetl*, the one eventually engraved in the Israeli collective memory, was an imaginary map and bore no similarity to the geographical and historical map of the place. Even superficial inspection of any one of the hundreds of maps that appear in the memorial books for the eastern European communities destroyed in the Holocaust will surprise those who were raised on the image of the *shtetl* as an all-Jewish place, separate and distinct from the gentile surroundings. In Leżajsk, for example, the great Bernardine Basilica stands not far from the town's synagogues and next door to the rabbi's house. Only several hundred paces separate this Catholic house of prayer, one of the holiest in Poland, from the grave of the saintly Rabbi Elimelech of Leżajsk. As Hasidim flocked to the *ohel* (mausoleum) of this *tsadik,* they encountered pious Poles on their way to the adjacent church. In Vilna, the most important synagogues were right next to an especially revered Catholic church. In this church, mentioned in the introduction to *Pan Tadeusz*, the epic by the great Polish poet Adam Mickiewicz,[10] Our Lady of Ostra Brama ("the High Gate") was venerated barely a stone's throw from the *shulhoif*—the city's synagogue courtyard.

---

9. On post–World War II demonic images of the Jews in rural Poland, see Alina Cała, *The Image of the Jew in Polish Folk Culture* (Jerusalem: Magnes, 1995), 112–83.

10. "Lithuania, my country, thou art like health; how much thou shouldst be prized only he can learn who has lost thee. To-day thy beauty in all its splendour I see and describe, for I yearn for thee. Holy Virgin, who protectest bright Czenstochowa and shinest above the Ostra Gate in Wilno!" (Adam Mickiewicz, *Pan Tadeusz, or the Last Foray in Lithuania, a Story of Life among Polish Gentlefolk in the Years 1811 and 1812, in Twelve Books*, trans. George Rappal Noyes (London and Toronto: J. M. Dent & Sons, 1917), 1.

The historian of eastern European Jewry is unsurprised by this prox-imity. Many *shtetlekh* in the Polish-Lithuanian Commonwealth grew up around an ancient core where the town's main institutions—including churches, synagogues, town hall, and market square with its shops—had clustered in previous centuries. The proximity of Christian and Jewish institutions did not lead to rapprochement or any significant cultural rela-tionship between those who visited them, despite daily contact in eco-nomic life. *"Der goy iz tref, ober zayn gelt is kosher"* (A *goy* is non-kosher but his money is kosher) went a common saying among the Jews of the east-ern European *shtetl*. The market square—in most *shtetlekh* a spacious, muddy vacant lot where peasants from surrounding villages parked their carts, a place bordered by wooden stalls laden with household wares, haberdashery, baked goods, and beverages—was the venue where Jews and gentiles mingled. It was typical for a Jew to lease a tavern from a Polish nobleman, and the tavern was almost the only place of amusement for peasants from the surrounding villages. It was so central in the tapes-try of relations among the various ethnic groups across eastern Europe that it took on supernatural significance in Christian villagers' eyes.[11] Until the second half of the nineteenth century, the manufacture, distribution, and sale of alcoholic beverages in eastern Europe was associated with *shtetl* Jews.

The world of Ashkenazi Judaism, created in central Europe and extended by constant migration into the heart of the Polish-Lithuanian Commonwealth, was largely also the world of Yiddish. This language, the language of the *shtetl*, transmitted ancient strata of traditions, linking Talmudic discourse with the experiences that the Jews had accumulated in their wanderings among the Christian kingdoms that had sprouted from the fragments of the western Roman Empire. In the *shtetl*, Yiddish, the vernacular of Ashkenazi Jews from Alsace in the west to Lithuania and the Ukraine in the east maintained the psychological boundaries that sep-arated the Jews from the Christians among whom they lived.

Many expressions familiar to us from the literature of medieval Jewish–Christian disputes remained alive and kicking in the daily vernac-ular of eastern European Jewry. A detailed lexicon of separation drew clear boundaries between the Jewish and Christian worlds. These linguis-tic borders strengthened what the reality of *shtetl* life weakened. For exam-ple, the Jew eats (*est*–עסט) and the non-Jew gorges (*frest*–פרעסט). The Jew is "one of ours" (*fun undzere*–פון אונדזערע) and the non-Jew is "one of theirs" (*fun zayere*–פון זייערע). The Jew has a house of prayer (*shul*–שול); the Christian

---

11. On the image of the rural Jewish tavern keeper in Poland, see Magdalena Opalski, *The Jewish Tavern-Keeper and His Tavern in Nineteenth-Century Polish Literature* (Jerusalem: Zalman Shazar Center, 1986); and Glenn Dynner, *Yankel's Tavern: Jews, Liquor, and Life in the Kingdom of Poland* (Oxford: Oxford University Press, 2014).

has a house of folly (*tifle*–תיפלה) or of impurity (*tume*–טומאה). The Jew has a festival (*ḥag*–חג); the *goy* has a day of terror (*khoge*—חגא). The non-Jew, in Yiddish, is a *shaygets* (שגץ) and his wife is a *shikse* (שיקסע), both words from the verse fragment *shaqets teshaqtsenu* ("שקץ תשקצנו") "surely you shall revile them" (Deuteronomy 7:26). Sometimes Jews even changed place-names to avoid uttering the word "church" in one of the local vernaculars! The Ukrainian town Belaya Tserkov (Russian: White Church), for example, was given the pejorative *Di shvartse tume* (Black Impurity)—but was usually called *Sadeh lavan* (White Field).[12]

Of course, the vernacular of the *shtetl* Jews had room not only for pejoratives, expressions of disgust, and the language of separation and distance. There were also one or two words and phrases of a different kind: *An erlekher goy* (a decent non-Jew) or *Vos far a khilk? A goy oder a yid, alts a mentsh* ("What's the difference? *Goy* or Jew, they're all people").

The new Hebrews in Palestine, wishing to replace the *shtetl* language with that of the Bible and to adopt a modernistic discourse of universal reform, removed many of the terms of segregation and separation from their lexicon. In the new Jewish memory of the Land of Israel, *the religious separation* that the *shtetl* had maintained between Christians and Jews and expressed in its venerable semantic tradition, was replaced by *ethno-national estrangement*. The *psychological distance* that had existed between Jews and non-Jews who lived next to each other was transformed into a memory of *physical-geographic isolation*. Jews in Palestine began to remember the faraway *shtetl* in eastern Europe as an impotent, inward-facing place that needed national revitalization and social revolution in order to withstand the violence of the surrounding majority populations.

Language was only one element in a complex set of symbols that drew the borders of the Jews' special identity in the multicultural world of eastern Europe. Every ethnic or religious group had its own ecology. The smell of fried lard, wafting from the homes of the Christians in the *shtetl*, both Catholics and Pravoslavic (Russian Orthodox); the fragrance of incense billowing from the churches; the strains of the organ; the chanting of the choir; and the pealing of the bells—all of these belonged to an alien world, a world that surrounded the Jews on all sides, close enough to touch, sometimes invading their backyards and always within eyeshot. This ecological experience, perhaps the most salient feature of the *shtetl* whence the founders of the New Yishuv in Palestine had come, did not take possession of the minds of the Israeli-born in its full strength; rather, it trickled into their consciousness through literary and ideological filters.

Historical reality, as stated, had very little in common with the literary image of the *shtetl*. The image, engraved on the new Palestinian Jewish

---

12. In order to avoid saying the forbidden "church," they used a "neutral" word.

collective memory, perpetuated the eastern European *shtetlekh* as Jewish islands in a non-Jewish sea that surrounded the *shtetl* on all sides but never broke in. In reality, the *shtetl* was never a Jewish-only place that existed in geographic and historical isolation. Jews lived there in very close physical proximity to Poles, Ukrainians, or Lithuanians. This proximity did not lead to spiritual rapprochement, as we said; neither, however, did it obliterate the ecological separation. On the contrary—perversely, the proximity of neighbors of the other faith made the difference in sounds, smells, and tastes much more salient. "Jacob" and "Esau" (*Eysev* was a common Yiddish term for a gentile) were absolute concepts that the eastern European experience bequeathed to the modern Jewish consciousness.

The separation that persisted in the historical *shtetl* was neither merely ecological nor solely psychological. The Jewish (and non-Jewish) inhabitants of this place experienced it as something cosmic: between the godly and the satanic, the pure and the impure, good deeds and evil deeds. In the ahistorical discourse that was an essential part of the cultural history of eastern European Jewry, Jacob and Esau in the homiletic literature became Jew and Ukrainian, Jew and Pole, and so on. Jacob and Esau, two brothers in the Yiddish folk song (available to Israeli-born boys and girls through the poet Ḥayim Naḥman Bialik's Hebrew translation), attempted unsuccessfully to transmit the power of this war of worlds to a new world composed of young Israelis. Here it is in English:

> Esau wakes up and heads for the tavern the shot glass in his mouth giving off its aroma.
>
> . . .
>
> Jacob wakes up and heads for the house of prayer to give praise and glory to his Creator.[13]

The song (in Yiddish) concludes as follows: "Oy, oy, oy, Esau is a *goy* / he's a drunkard / he's got to drink / after all, he's a *goy* (*Oy, oy, oy, Eysev iz a goy / shikkr iz er / trinkn muz er / vayl er iz a goy*"). I myself can remember that worshipers sang this ditty (in Yiddish!) after *kiddush* at an old synagogue in the heart of Tel Aviv—the new Zionist city—in the late 1950s, on my bar mitzvah day.

Some Jews crossed the *shtetl*'s internal borders to the other side. The physical distance was very small: sometimes one had only to traverse the lane that separated the courtyard of the great synagogue to the courtyard of the monastery next door. Conversions from Judaism were not rare in

---

13. Ḥayim Naḥman Bialik, "Ya'acov and Eysav" (Jacob and Esau), in *Kitvey H. N. Bialik*, vol. 1 (Tel Aviv: Va'ad ha-yovel, 1933), 228.

eastern Europe in the Middle Ages as they are in the modern era. Etched into the collective memory of eastern European Jewry was the Jewish tavern keeper's daughter who eloped with the Christian son of the Polish nobleman and embraced his religion. Conversion was sometimes kept secret (even though secrets were hard to keep in the *shtetl)* because the ghastly event dishonored the entire family. A Jew who lost a child to the church mourned as for a death.

The Jews' fear of apostasy revealed their dread of Christianity's powerful allure. The Christianization of a member of a pedigreed family was concealed to the greatest possible extent. The Chabad Hasidim did their very best to cover up their awareness that Reb Moshe, son of the founder of Chabad, R. Shneor Zalman of Liadi, had gone over to Christianity. The few Maskilim who lived in the eastern European *shtetlekh*, in contrast, did whatever they could to publicize this event in order to excoriate their bête noire, the Hasidic movement.[14]

For the Jews of the eastern European *shtetl*, Christianity was dark and threatening but also tempting. The attractiveness of the other faith was quite often material or social in nature. In the historical Kingdom of Poland, the state that vanished at the end of the eighteenth century, a Jew who opted for Catholicism could even join the nobility. This was a real incentive: overnight a Jew could shed his inferior and downtrodden status and attain the pinnacle of Polish society! In the Tsarist empire, conversion often carried the promise of an academic post or a promotion in the civil service.

In the collective memory of eastern European Jewry, apostates lived on either as traitors to their people or as faithful to their Jewishness. Jacob Brafman (1824–1879), author of the infamous *Kahal Book* (a translation of excerpts from the Minsk community records that ostensibly disclosed what the Jews really thought about the non-Jews), was an apostate. Constantin Abba Shapiro (1839–1900), a pioneer of the Ḥibat Tsiyon movement in Russia, was also an apostate but is fondly remembered because he continued to support the Jewish national movement. His nationalistic Hebrew poems were very popular among the early Jewish settlers in Palestine.[15]

In the memory of the immigrants to Palestine, the allure of Christianity metamorphosed from a religious issue into an ethnocultural tension between a violent and threatening majority and a persecuted and powerless minority. In this respect as well, the new Hebrew literature wielded

---

14. David Assaf, *Untold Tales of the Hasidim: Crisis & Discontent in the History of Hasidism*, Tauber Institute for the Study of European Jewry Series (Waltham, MA: Brandeis University Press, 2010), 29–96.

15. We should not forget, however, that in not a few cases conversion to Christianity took place for reasons of inner conviction or mystical attraction.

great power by exporting a dual image of the *shtetl* to Palestine: decaying, antiquated, flaccid—but also an island of pure Jewish life amid a sea of violent strangers. The weaker the radical ideologies that sought to distance themselves from the *shtetl* became, the stronger became the nostalgic image of an integral and unsullied Jewish world, totally separate from its gentile environment.

The either-or separation projected by the spirit of the Ashkenazi legacy intersected marvelously with the new national discourse even though it did not resemble it in every respect. In the daily life of the *shtetl* Jew, however—a life that rarely corresponded with the collective national memory—there were also other kinds of *goyim*, who projected the opposite of cosmic separation. The coexistence, good relations, and human proximity that one could find between Jews and their neighbors in the *shtetl* were inconsistent with the image of wretched exile shaped by the good old Zionist education that the Palestine-born Jews received in the Mandate era and in Israel's first years. In that portrayal of *shtetl* life, pogroms raged, blood libels unfolded, the *goy* threatened, and the church cast its frightening shadow. All of this, adapted to the new radical nationalist discourse, became fixed in several generations of Israeli collective memory. The parts of the story that were not transferred to the new discourse, or at least were not underscored, were the nonconflictual channels of relations between Jews and members of the nations among which they had settled. In the *shtetl*, in fact, the Jews felt like members of the dominant population. Therefore, their fear of the surroundings was accompanied by a sense of control of the urban space.

This sense reflected the uniqueness of the eastern European Jewish demography: Jews accounted for an important share of their towns' population but were a minority of the total population of the countries where they lived. In many *shtetlekh*, they were sometimes an absolute majority. In these places, they could sustain a worldview in which the non-Jew resided on the fringes of Jewish life. The Judaized *goy*, a Christian by confession, who absorbed something of the town's dominant culture, was a regular fixture in the *shtetlekh* of eastern Europe. The *shabbes goy*, a member of the lower social classes, was an essential institution and a permanent member of the Jewish household. He performed a set of forbidden labors on the Sabbath in return—as the practice had it—for a slice of the Sabbath bread, a hunk of fish from the Sabbath table, and a shot of brandy. The affluent sometimes had a live-in *goya* (female goy) who was well versed in the rules of keeping kosher, spoke Yiddish, and even rushed the children off to synagogue and nagged them to say their blessings. In fact, the *shabbes goy* and the Christian nanny were much more common in the *shtetl* than the pogrom and the blood libel. Nonetheless, the Jewish national rebirth in the Land of Israel seems to have had no need to remember them.

What survived from the complex ethnic makeup of the real *shtetl* was the memory of fear, threat, and tension between Israel and the other nations.

The universe of the Jewish *shtetl*, with its Jews, its *goyim*, and their common ground, has been almost totally obliterated, and its vestiges are steadily being expunged from the contemporary Jewish collective memory. The Yiddish language, a definitive player in imparting the memory of the eastern European past, has surrendered its primacy to other languages. What remains of the *shtetl* today is an anachronistic image that draws on a jumble of ideologies in literary debate, motion pictures, television shows, cyberspace, and a steadily vanishing folklore. In Israel today, the image of the *shtetl* resembles the one commonly found in the United States: Marc Chagall and *Fiddler on the Roof.*

Even the ultra-Orthodox Jews, the so-called *Haredim,* ostensibly those closest to the spirit of this vanished world, have invented their very own *shtetl*—an Orthodox *shtetl* in the spirit of the twenty-first century. In the more secular Israeli consciousness, the clanging church bells, the pogrom, and the *shtetl* market square have merged with the all-consuming and all-transformative memory of the Holocaust. Who in Israel today still knows about the Christian nanny who recited the *modeh ani* (morning prayer of gratitude) with the Jewish *shtetl* householder's children? Who remembers the *shtetl* apostate? Who in Tel Aviv, or even in Jerusalem, imagines that the rabbi's home and the priest's residence in the *shtetl* were sometimes on the opposite sides of a fence? Israelis do retain memories of being scared of the European *goy,* or at least they have heard that this fear once existed. The fear itself has gone away or has been so deeply repressed beneath the threshold of consciousness that even the pealing of church bells and the fragrance of the incense no longer arouse it.

6

Lubavitch, Berlin, and Kinneret:
From the "Science of Judaism"
to the "Science of Zionism"

The New Yishuv, which emerged in late Ottoman and early Mandate Palestine, was not built only by Jewish farmers and laborers. A small but influential group of intellectuals also played a significant role in this enterprise. Writers, poets, teachers, and newspaper editors, along with amateur geographers, archaeologists, and historians, helped shape the infrastructure for a new national culture in Palestine. This culture, which was to become a principal element in Israeli identity, is unprecedented in Jewish history. While its roots lie in the Jewish renewal movements that emerged and developed in Europe in the century preceding the First Aliyah, this culture is unique in that it combines attachment to Eretz Yisrael (the Land of Israel) with concepts, values, and outlooks absorbed from modern European culture.

Eretz Yisrael was a central component in the belief system of traditional Jewish society: over the generations, the memory of the Land of Israel accompanied Jewish believers in their daily prayers. Its hills and valleys, streams and springs, and fruits and vegetables were an inseparable part of the religious calendar, constantly commemorated on the holidays and days of mourning. The holy texts that the Jews studied were replete with stories of the ancient Land of Israel, with images of its days of glory, and with heart-rending descriptions of its destruction.

Innovative Western ideas were espoused mainly by the Haskalah movement, but other modernistic currents also flowed strongly within the Jewish communities of nineteenth-century Europe and the Mediterranean basin. In them, social doctrines, political theories, and economic models from the Enlightenment heritage of eighteenth-century Europe combined with the influences of German, French, and British Romanticism, the platforms of national movements in central and eastern Europe, and ideas for the perfection of humankind and a world of political and social radicalism.

However, the creation of an attachment to the Holy Land with tools appropriated from the Western conceptual world was a radical turning point—one that established a strong similarity between nationalist Jewish intellectuals and corresponding groups in the national movements of other central and eastern European ethnic groups. In this chapter, I will examine one star in this constellation of national-minded intellectuals— Zalman Shazar-Rubashov (1889–1974), a Zionist historian and political functionary who had been born a Hasidic Jew but later became a socialist and eventually the third president of the State of Israel. By tracing the way this historian sought to translate the traditional language of previous generations into the discourse of the nineteenth-century European national movements, we will uncover more of the tangled roots of the new Israeli culture. Shazar's ideas had an enormous influence on the nascent Hebrew culture in Palestine, due to his many years as an editor, publisher, educator, and speaker. He was a Labor Zionist cultural entrepreneur, whose activity reached out to tens of thousands of workers, boys and girls in youth movements, and members of the Haganah, the Jewish paramilitary organization. Shazar later served as the editor-in-chief of the leading Israeli daily *Davar* from 1944 to 1949.

In 1971, a hefty Hebrew volume titled *Orei Dorot* (Lights of Bygone Generations) appeared, containing a selection of academic articles and lectures on Jewish history by Shazar-Rubashov. Included in the volume were historical studies and essays published in Hebrew as well as translations of articles originally written in Yiddish and German over a period of more than fifty years, from the 1910s to the early 1960s. During those years, the Zionist-Socialist Shazar managed to be arrested by the Tsarist police for subversive political activity, to study history and philosophy in Germany, and to immigrate to Palestine, where he played an important role in the political and cultural life of the emerging Zionist community and in shaping the new Hebrew culture. In the first years of the State of Israel, Shazar served as Minister of Education and Culture, and in this capacity his approach to Jewish history and culture was put to the test in response to the challenges of absorbing the huge wave of immigration, in which hundreds of thousands of Jews arrived from different cultural communities.

Following Shazar's way of thinking, the editors of *Orei Dorot* claimed to be repatriating the aged author's historical writings from their scattered lands of exile to their home (Hebrew: *ligvulam*).[1] They did so by collecting the writing that was not yet accessible to Israeli readers whose first language was Hebrew, thereby adding another layer to what was known as the national ingathering project (also *mif'al ha-kinus*).[2] In the preface to the

---

1. *Ligvulam* metaphorically means "to their own territory."
2. Parenthetically, I played a minor role in preparing this book for press. The late Professor Israel Halpern (1910–1971) of the Hebrew University, a scholar of eastern European Jewish history, was one of the editors; as his research assistant, I checked references to the

volume, the elderly Zionist historian Benzion Dinur (1884–1973)—also Minister of Education in Israel's early years—described Shazar's way of practicing the historian's craft:

> This author, scholar, and lecturer [Shazar] wants to introduce his readers and audience to four "eras" while apprising them of the "whole" that he sees in them: (1) the hopes and philosophy of redemption; (2) the settlement and shape of The Land of Israel; (3) the sufferings of the scattered and persecuted [Jewish] people; (4) the struggle for its survival and form; and [Jewry's] entrance into and struggle with modern culture and society in Europe.[3]

With these words Dinur, a founding father of the Zionist school in historiography—commonly known as the Jerusalem School—was defining the place of another Zionist historian, then serving as the third president of the State of Israel, in the circle of national historians. Indeed, anyone who reads this volume of studies and essays and is well versed in the concepts and scholarly methodology of the Jerusalem School will immediately be aware of Shazar's profound connection to it. It surfaces, sharply and clearly, in the themes that Shazar chose, the methodological background of his works, and his writing style. Above all, it is evident in the explicit and unabashed convergence of ideology, politics, and historical scholarship visible on almost every page in the anthology.

In his autobiographical work *Morning Stars* (Hebrew: *kokhvei boker*), Shazar tellingly expressed the essence of his view concerning the strong connection between history and nationalism, writing as a historian who devoted most of his life to movement politics: "I would not, [he said], teach anything about the future of the nation before trying to elucidate for myself, scientifically, the struggles of the Jewish past."[4]

At the beginning of an article about Rabbi David Conforti, a seventeenth-century Jewish chronicler and a contemporary of Shabbetai Zevi (the Sephardic kabbalist who claimed to be the long-awaited Jewish Messiah), published in Berlin in 1928,[5] Shazar wrote:

---

sources quoted in the book. I remember one German-language article in particular, "The Wheel of Fate of History," published in Germany in 1916 in the Zionist journal *Ost und West*; it was my job to track down references to sources and studies lacking in the original version of the article.

3. Benzion Dinur, "Preface," in Zalman Shazar, *Orei Dorot: Studies and Insights on Jewish History in Recent Generations* [Hebrew] (Jerusalem, 1971), 5–6.

4. Zalman Shazar, *Morning Stars*, trans. Shulamith Schwartz Nardi (Philadelphia: Jewish Publication Society of America, 1967); Hebrew original, *Kokhvei boker* (Tel Aviv: Am Oved, 1966). Here translated from the Hebrew original, p. 242.

5. Shazar, "The Author of *Qore hadorot* and His Time: A Biography of R. David Conforti" [Hebrew], *Ha-goren* 10 (1928): 122–32; reprinted in *Orei Dorot*, 96–106, here 96.

The spiritual world and living conditions of the researchers of Jewish history in the nineteenth and twentieth centuries is an open book for us. Knowing their areas of activity, their aptitudes, and their ways of thinking, we can also identify the origins of their interest in past issues and the connection between their attitude toward contemporary events and their grasp of eternal questions. Such is not the case with those who occasionally arose in the firmament of our lengthy Middle Ages to interpret past times, from Flavius Josephus to Marcus Jost.[6]

With his keen sense of history, this socialist Zionist, who had acquired academic training at several German universities, discerned the pronouncedly subjective nature of historiography—any historiography—and the need to understand correctly the motives of historians—including Jewish historians. He understood well—so at least he believed—the Jewish-German and Jewish-Russian modernist exponents of the *Wissenschaft* (i.e., science—the scientific study of Judaism and Jewish history), whose views he adhered to and rebelled against to varying degrees. Unlike the mid-nineteenth-century German Jewish *Wissenschaft* scholars, however, who claimed that modern Jewish historiography began only with the historical writings of Isaak Markus Jost (1793–1860), Shazar found elements of "national" (and, therefore, also "modern") historiography in the works of scholars of the early modern era.

His keen interest in the history of the seventeenth-century Sabbatean movement, which he considered the epitome of a national movement that failed and withered, prompted him to ponder the relationship between pre-*Wissenschaft* scholars of Jewish history and the objects of their research. Indeed, he often asked himself where this historical writing fit into the cultural-political tapestry of his time.

Thus it was that in his critical study of *Qore hadorot*, the chronicle produced by Conforti, Shazar reached a conclusion motivated by nationalism, arguing that it was nothing less than a historiographic response to the crisis of the Sabbatean messianic movement!

At the very height of the national disillusionment, R. David Conforti set forth to examine the history of his people as best he could, by delving into the historical chronicles that preceded him and such books and manuscripts as came into his possession. Linking one generation to the next, he strove to establish for himself and those around him the eternal chain of his nation, which had been shaken to its foundations by the self-falsification of its chosen redeemer [Shabbetai Zevi—Ed.] and the realization that the movement in which it had hoped was a fraud.[7]

---

6. Ibid., 96.
7. Ibid., 103.

By background, an *Ostjude* and a socialist Zionist who belonged to the large group of Jewish émigrés from Imperial Russia who had gathered in Berlin in the early twentieth century, Shazar himself was exposed to the vast social and cultural changes that German Jewry was undergoing. The choices of specific historical episodes in German Jewish history, and the historical interpretation that he gave these changes in his writings, were another expression of his strong association with the Zionist historical school.

For example, he displayed a special interest in the history of the *Verein für Kultur und Wissenschaft der Juden*, the scholarly society of young Jews in Prussia that historians consider the progenitor of *Wissenschaft des Judentums* in Germany.[8] A leitmotif in all his historical studies was the unity of the Jewish diaspora generally, and of the Ashkenazi diaspora in particular. Shazar regarded Ashkenazi Jewry as a national and cultural whole, bound by their religious ritual, vernacular, and mode of community organization. In this regard, his Zionist position converged with radical eastern European nationalism, Yiddishism, and the neo-Romanticism of the eastern European Jewish Left, which sought Jewish national elements in folk culture and the lives of lower-class folk strata.

Decades would pass before Israel Halpern, another important member of the Jerusalem School (and himself a socialist Zionist), would develop Shazar's view in his classic article, "Panic Marriages in Eastern Europe" (1962). In it he demonstrated the unity of traditional Jewish society by showing that the partitions of Poland (1772–1793) had little or no influence on the Jews, who had become Prussian, Austrian, and Russian subjects: "Here we discover Jewish society in Poland and partitioned Poland, divided among itself and fragmented between three kingdoms, as one living entity whose every fiber responded again and again, reflexively and invariably, to any attempt to attack its ways of life and traditional values."[9]

---

8. On the contribution of the Verein to modern Judaic scholarship, see Ismar Schorsch, *From Text to Context: The Turn to History in Modern Judaism*, Tauber Institute for the Study of European Jewry Series (Hanover, NH: University Press of New England, 1994), 205-32.

9. Israel Halpern, "Panic Marriages in Eastern Europe," *Eastern European Jewry: Historical Studies* [Hebrew], ed. Israel Halpern (Jerusalem: Magnes, 1968), 289–309, here 309. Halpern's essay describes a unique social phenomenon: an increase in child marriages as a spontaneous reaction to legislation passed by the absolutist regimes in Prussia, Russia, and Austria, which was aimed at restricting marriages and lowering the Jewish birth rate in the divided Polish–Lithuanian Commonwealth. In a comment appended after the essay was first published, Halpern added a very interesting piece of information regarding the continuation of this phenomenon in the end of the nineteenth century as well: In the time of the 1881–1882 pogroms, a rumor spread among the Jews of Tsarist Russia that the authorities were set to forbid marriage of all those under the age of twenty-two. Some parents were frightened and rushed to marry off their sons and daughters. In other words, this cross-border custom was still in existence when the modern Jewish national movement was beginning to awaken in eastern Europe.

In his 1929 paper on early-modern Yiddish-language testimonies in Ashkenazi *responsa* (Jewish legal decisions) as a historical source for the study of Jewish culture, Shazar wrote:

> They reflect a vernacular that survived uninterruptedly for several centuries in all the lands and territories where Yiddish was spoken. Not for nothing did B. Borochov[10]—in the very first years of his activity in linguistic research— ... state the rule: if we wish, nevertheless, to get an idea of the Yiddish vernacular at the time, the literature of the day will not enlighten us in any way. We must resort to the few documents that have survived from that time—by and large, testimonies given in rabbinic litigation and recorded in responsa (*Der Pinkes*, Vilna, 1913). To some extent, the honoring of B. Borochov's will is the purpose of this work of ours.[11]

Here, Shazar was describing his research project, the collection and publication of sources from communities in early modern Germany, Bohemia, Poland, and Lithuania, as executing the will of Ber Borochov, a major Marxist Zionist leader who was also a pioneer in the scholarly research of Yiddish! In other words, Shazar was projecting concepts of neo-Romantic nationalism and Zionist socialism onto rabbinical material produced by the ramified Jewish legal network that spanned central and eastern Europe in the early modern era. In the material that he gathered, he revealed a shared folk culture that could not otherwise be found because it had been buried in the texts written by the ruling elites.

Much like Halpern, who would later exhume from literary and rabbinic sources a spontaneous folk practice—marrying off children in response to legislation from the centralized regime—Shazar sought in the testimonies that he gathered, a spontaneous folk language that, to his mind, reflected the national unity of the dispersed Ashkenazi masses.

What, however, had been the fate of this unity, with its quintessential national markers, that had existed in the pre-national era? As did many Jewish intellectuals of eastern European origin who succumbed to the charms of German culture, Shazar identified what he saw as anti-national tendencies in the Jewish–German encounter at the onset of modernity. To him, the wedge that the late eighteenth century partitioning of Poland drove between the two sections of the Ashkenazi diaspora—the "western" and the "eastern"—should be interpreted in a way quite different from that of the German *Wissenschaft des Judentums* as exemplified by the historians Markus Jost and Heinrich Graetz, who considered Polish-Lithuanian

---

10. Ber Borochov (1881–1917) was a radical Jewish labor Zionist leader and thinker. He was a committed Yiddishist and Yiddish philologist now recognized as the founder of modern Yiddish studies in eastern Europe.—IB.

11. Shazar, "Yiddish Testimonies in 15th–17th Centuries Responsa" [Hebrew], *Orei Dorot*, 239–319, here 242.

Jewry a withered and outdated appendage of Ashkenazi Jewry. These historians viewed the *Ostjuden* as unfortunate brethren who had not yet been privileged to bask in the blessed sunlight of the Enlightenment and the tidings of the Emancipation. Moreover, they regarded them, in all those places to which they migrated from the east, as a threat to progress and to Jewish–Christian rapprochement.

Shazar, a loyal successor to the group of Jewish historians from Imperial Russia, rebelled against this German Jewish hegemony and turned the picture upside-down: in the national history that he wrote, the *Westjuden* were the villains and the *Ostjuden* were the good guys. Everything that German Jewish historiography condemned and rejected—or at least presented as antiquated and backward in terms of the innovations of the time—scored well on Shazar's scale of national values. In the spirit of Russian Jewish historian Simon Dubnow (1860–1941), his mentor in investigating premodern Jewish autonomy, Shazar discerned two types of struggle for emancipation in Ashkenazi society. The emancipation in western Europe was marked by assimilation, a legacy of Sephardi Jewry in pre-Revolutionary France that German Jewry also embraced. The emancipation in eastern Europe, however, was cut from very different cloth. Thus, Shazar wrote in 1916:

> The transition of various areas in Eastern Europe to constitutional democracy and civil liberty encounters a Jewish public that has no connection whatsoever to the ideology of De Pinto.[12] Indeed, the past century has raised the Jews' national lives, creative endeavors, and hopes in this region to such a high level that it should be considered one of the pinnacles in Diaspora history. Accordingly, the emancipation of these Oriental Jews (Hebrew: *yehudei hamizrah*) [no less!—Ed.] is distinct from the French example, just as this flourishing spring of Jewish culture is distant, and as remote, from the lifeless desert of the disconnected conversos of Bordeaux.[13]

Shazar thus saw a powerful reserve of vitality in eastern European Jewry, which had retained its national culture and its languages, customs, and ways of life until the turn of the twentieth century. The national consciousness that many Jews in the communities of western and central Europe had lost in the modern era appeared, to him, to be thriving among their brethren in the eastern part of the continent. He went so far as to propose an explanation for the preservation of the national character of the great

---

12. Isaac de Pinto (1717–1787) was a Dutch Jewish writer and patrician of Portuguese origin. In his *Apologie pour la Nation Juive, ou Réflexions Critiques* (Amsterdam: Chez J. Joubert, 1762) De Pinto defended his co-religionists against Voltaire's polemical attacks.—IB.

13. Shazar, "Assimilation and Emancipation," *Orei Dorot*, 230–34, here 234.

Jewish collective in eastern Europe à la Dubnow:[14] The Jews in the Polish-Lithuanian Commonwealth had enjoyed well-developed and strong autonomy, with official recognition and cooperation; this autonomy underpinned a national entity that existed before the obliteration of Polish independence—and endured after partition too.

Beyond even that, the old Polish-Lithuanian Commonwealth, which upheld the autonomy of diverse ethnic groups and refrained from meddling in their internal affairs, played an immensely important role in fortifying the pronouncedly national identity of eastern European Jewry. What happened after the partitioning of Poland, that is, from the late eighteenth century onward, according to Shazar, was that two trends foreign to the legacy of the Polish-Lithuanian Commonwealth developed on what had been the territory of Poland. On the one hand, the conservative wing of Polish nationalism advocated the removal of the Jews from economic life and non-Jewish society. On the other hand, those of the liberal persuasion embraced the Emancipationist stance. Inspired by the principles of the French Revolution, they argued that Jewish autonomy should be totally abolished and the Jews should be assimilated into Polish culture. Thus, wrote Shazar in 1916, at a time when the future status of the Jews in the multinational empires after the end of World War I was an issue of concern to many: "These two trends have maintained their dominance in Polish public life all those years. Rejection or assimilation, excommunication or separation—these were the only alternatives offered the enslaved Jews of Poland. This—if we may invoke the language of Jewish history here—was the voice of exilic Polonized Jewry."[15]

If so, early modern Poland spawned the very same ethnocultural entity that the *Wissenschaft*-minded historians rejected—the one that the Jewish national historians, including Shazar, portrayed as the cradle of national existence in the past, present, and future. The national strength of eastern European Jewry outlasted the exclusionist forces applied from without by the centralized state and from within by the Jewish elites:

> The Polish people never ceased to be a people even after the Polish state ceased to exist. Similarly, the Jewish people did not shed its national character even after Jewish autonomy was liquidated. The aim of assimilating the Jews into Polish culture failed, just as the aim of assimilating

---

14. For Dubnow's ideas on premodern Jewish nationalism in eastern Europe, see Israel Bartal, "'A Substitute for a Government, for a State and for Citizenship': Simon Dubnow's Image of Medieval Autonomy," *A Missionary for History: Essays in Honor of Simon Dubnov*, ed. Abraham Greenbaum and Kristi Groberg, Minnesota Mediterranean and East European Monographs 7 (Minneapolis: University of Minnesota Press, 1998), 11–18.

15. Shazar, "Jewish Autonomy in Independent Poland," *Orei Dorot*, 212–21, here 220.

the Poles into German and Russian culture failed, with the exception of a narrow stratum of deserters and traitors.[16]

In stressing the similarity, if not the parallel, of Polish nationalism and Jewish nationalism, Shazar was anticipating something like a future restoration of the reality in pre-partition eastern Europe: both nations would reestablish a relationship based on recognition of national minority rights. Prompted by his dialectical historical thinking, Shazar thus viewed the awakening of the Jewish national movement in the late nineteenth century (and of Polish nationalism at the same time) as a rejuvenated and fresh product of a merger between the Jewish community's national character from before the demise of Polish independence and the influences of modernity:

> The Jews' spiritual culture has definitely been renewed but the national character of this culture has lost none of its potency. Both the Polish people and the Jewish public are national blocs that are historically singular and have retained enough strength from their past to vigorously resist any attempt at coercion. And just as any new political constellation will naturally reawaken the Polish people's old hopes for the resurrection of its national independence, so by necessity, and in organic fashion, will the Jews' aspiration to resurrect their right to self-determination within the same country be awakened.[17]

The Shazar of the World War I era was so captivated by autonomist (not to say "Dubnovian") ideas that in his thinking he managed to meld the concept of Jewish autonomy in the Polish-Lithuanian Commonwealth with the Jews' preservation of the connection with the Land of Israel and aspirations to political redemption there![18] On the nexus of autonomy, which by nature is parochial and limited to the confines of an individual state, district, or community, and the transnational channels that linked Jews of different diasporas, he argued, "The logical conclusion of autonomy is that only under its auspices does the singular national nature of the people develop freely. The idea of pan-Jewish solidarity and the longing for redemption are the main indicators of the singular Jewish national nature."[19]

Then, with some pathos, the critical historian ventured into the realms

---

16. Ibid.

17. Ibid., 220–21.

18. Jewish Autonomists in Eastern Europe in the late 19th and early 20th century believed in viability of Jewish diaspora as long as Jewish communities maintain self-rule, and rejected assimilation. Autonomism was adopted in the platforms of several radical Jewish parties such as the Bund. Some political thinkers, like Shazar blended Autonomism with Zionism .

19. Shazar, "Jewish Autonomy," 217.

of the imagination and, going well beyond what the sources in our possession actually say or even imply, he amplified the role played by the Council of the Four Lands, the overarching communal organization of Polish
Jewry (dissolved in 1764), in Jewish messianic movements and fund-
raising drives for the Jews of Palestine. Thus, wrote Shazar in a burst of
national passion:

> If the detailed minutes of the Council's meetings were in our possession,
> we would certainly read at the end of the Chair's opening and conclud-
> ing speeches the traditional verse, replete with longing: "A redeemer will
> come to Zion." The sermons of R. Ephraim of Lenczica and R. Berechia
> the Preacher, given during the meetings at the Council's synagogue, are
> adequate evidence of this.[20]

As long as Shazar the historian dealt with premodern Jewish society generally and the great eastern European Jewish collective particularly, it was
not difficult for him, like any other Jewish nationally minded historian, to
judge the Jewish past with standards drawn from modern national discourse. After all, the premodern ethnoreligious Jewish communities had
preserved markers of singularity, languages, and customs, and they had
staunchly cultivated a consciousness of continuity that transcended time
and place.

Things were different when it came to the Jews' transition from the
early modern corporative society to the modern era. Being a modernist
flush with radical political views who also maintained a solid nationalist
outlook, Shazar—much like other members of the Zionist school in historiography—resorted to dialectic explanations of Jewish modernity. He
was able to integrate the most radical of radicals—those who wanted to
utterly negate the Jews' separate existence and merge the moribund Jewish corporation into a future classless society—into his new historical nar-
rative alongside advocates of Jewish continuity and the Jews' preservation
of their ethnic-religious heritage.

He managed, for example, to integrate Jewish thinkers who were
among the leading exponents of radical universalism into the dialectic
push-and-pull, which he sought to uncover in the history of the encounter
with modernity a move that yielded a seeming unity of national and social
radicalism. Thus, Shazar interpreted the turn to virulent anti-Judaism in
the thought of the German-Jewish socialist Ferdinand Lassalle (1825–1864)
as an early manifestation of the revolution of consciousness that Zionism
triggered among the Jews of Germany! In an article published in Tel Aviv
in 1926, when the Zionist labor movement marked the centenary of

---

20. Ibid., 208.

Lassalle's birth, Shazar quoted a letter written by Lassalle to his father that reeked of hatred for Judaism and Jews. Shazar pathetically stated:

> Thus, the fate [of the Jews] was sealed. These were the first words uttered in the uprising against the weakness of our downtrodden status [as Jews]. For their own generation—the end of betrayal; and for posterity —the onset of the uprising. Many days would pass, new forces would surge forth until, finally, it burst through the seams. And Lasalle, this man once banished from the Jewish tent, would rise up to be purified in the crucible of [future] generations, becoming Israel's sharpened sword in its war for dignity, fulfilling his youthful wish.[21]

Little surprise then that Ferdinand Lassalle, like other radical leaders of Jewish descent, was successfully integrated into the new collective memory that the Zionist intellectuals wished to shape for the consumers of the new Hebrew culture in the Land of Israel. At least two large cities in contemporary Israel—Tel Aviv and Holon—have streets bearing Lassalle's name. This is a remnant of the days when the Hebrew national project imported the heritage of Jewish revolutionaries into the Land of the Fathers and took care that their memory would not be expunged from the Zionist story. [22] This interpretative line brings to mind the charged and troubling dialogue between modern antisemitism and nineteenth-century Jewish national thinking, which several *Jerusalem School* historians (e.g., Shmuel Almog, 1926–2008) have pointed out.[23] Note the striking similarity between the way the radical national historian integrated the so-called wild offshoots of Sabbateanism (Hebrew: *sfiḥei hashabbta'ut*) into his grand historical tableau, and the way he embedded Jewish radicalism at the time of the struggle for emancipation in the very same picture. In Shazar's mind both the failed early-modern messianic movement that had metamorphosed into a mélange of underground sects and the German Jewish revolutionaries of the nineteenth century tilted Jewish national energy away from the mainstream of their history.

---

21. Shazar, "Ferdinand Lassalle, the German Jew," *Orei dorot*, 334–46, here 346.

22. The combination of Jewish nationalism and social radicalism was an unmistakable, distinctive mark of the culture that the eastern European immigrants developed overseas. It is interesting to point out that a hundred years ago, the memory of Lassalle among American Jewry was quite similar to his memory in Israel. A ten-story building with an eye-catching front stands at 175 East Broadway in New York City; above the entrance to the building, an embossed inscription testifies that in this building resided the editorial board of the Yiddish socialist newspaper *Forverts* (Forward). The building's façade, which was completed in 1912, presents reliefs of important figures in world socialism, including Karl Marx and Ferdinand Lassalle.

23. Shmuel Almog, "Between Zionism and Antisemitism," *Patterns of Prejudice* 28.2 (1994): 49–59.

At the end of this dialectical *démarche*, however, both national currents reverted to their correct course, that of Zionist redemption in Palestine. There can be no more open expression of the astonishing connection between the memory of the eighteenth-century Frankists, passionate believers in redemption who slid out of the Jewish mainstream into what many considered "convoluted paths and befouled clearings,"[24] and the memory of the German Jewish revolutionaries and world reformers, than the following remarks made by Shazar in the centenary year of Karl Marx's birth, 1918. When Shazar penned them, just a handful of Second Aliyah (1904–1914) socialist immigrants remained in Palestine and were beginning to recover from the devastation of World War I. These people, young men and women who had come to the Land of Israel during the last decade of Ottoman rule were the social-political core from which the ruling elite of the Yishuv would emerge in the following decades, during the British Mandate and the first days of the State of Israel.

It was of them that the historian-seer wrote:

> How did a gentile philosophy of purely non-Jewish origin [i.e., Marxism], which managed to weave itself so deeply into the tangle of all our prob-lems and tasks, find a way to couple with the very soul of our struggles and hopes and to return to our people's innermost sanctum? Does the whole thing not prove that the entire philosophy is not really of non-Jew-ish origin? A hidden path leads from the burning rage that the Jewish prophets directed at rulers and oppressors to the wellspring of Karl Marx's dream. It leads from the crucible of the Jewish saints' rock-solid faith in the dominion of divine justice in history. It leads from the medi-eval mystics' superhuman faith in the fulfillment of the messianic idea, and from there slowly meanders, through destructions and indignities, through enlightenment and assimilation. It leads from the frigid hatred that surfaces in Marx's hostile and hurtful libel [a reference to Marx's famous 1844 article, "On the Jewish Question"] ... and the cold cellar of Bund's "neutralism," up to the struggle for redemption evidenced in the sun-induced creases in the faces of the Jewish worker and guardsman in the Land of Israel. The road from Marx's libel winds steadily back to Jewish reality.[25]

This was indeed a remarkable essay that coupled the mystical messiahs of the seventeenth and eighteenth centuries with the socialist revolutionaries of the nineteenth and twentieth centuries as part of the process leading to Zionist rebirth.

---

24. Here Shazar refers to the radical antinomian theology preached by Jacob Frank, a theology Shazar understood as a blunt diversion from the traditional Jewish expectation for redemption.

25. Shazar, "Marx on Judaism and Judaism in Marx," *Orei dorot*, 320–33, here 333.

Zalman Shazar was an epitome of the school of Jewish historians who were born out of the political-cultural encounter between the central European *Wissenschaft* and the national awakening in the multiethnic empires of eastern Europe. His research on Jewish history nourished his political activity and vice versa. From the legacy of the *Wissenschaft des Judentums* and German historiography, he appropriated the methodology and the integration of philosophy and history; from the intellectual environment and the political ferment of Imperial Russia, he imbibed the influences of social radicalism and national neo-Romanticism. In varying proportions and emphases, this combination was typical of the scholarship and public activity of dozens of Jewish historians who were born in Imperial Russia and the Hapsburg Empire in the last decades of the nineteenth century. Many of them acquired their academic training at German or Polish universities, joined one of the modern national movements that blossomed on the eve of World War I, and experienced the subsequent collapse of the Imperial order and the ascendancy of the postwar nation-states.

The Zionist school of historiography was an extension of this "Historians International," which established itself in Palestine, placed the Land of Israel at the center of Jewish history, and appropriated the national cultural assets that had been created over the centuries throughout the diaspora. In 1945, Zalman Shazar, the socialist Zionist historian and member of the Zionist labor movement in Palestine—stunned by reports about the extent of the Holocaust in Europe and enthralled by the flourishing Yishuv enterprise in the Middle East at the end of the Second World War—stepped forward to take stock of *Wissenschaft des Judentums*. He presented the thrilling historical development that national historiography had revealed, highlighting the Jewish people's metamorphoses from exile to revival.

This path of development was, following a major Jerusalem School convention, dialectical. It took shape in the responses of the Lovers of Zion (*Hovevei Tsiyon*) to the pogroms that swept the southern provinces of Imperial Russia in 1881–1882. According to Shazar, it began with the supremely optimistic encounter between members of the Jewish traditional communities and European culture, continued with vacillations in light of the Jews' incomplete integration into the surrounding societies, and culminated in rejection, repulsion, and departure. In Shazar's words, "For our wretched, audacious generation, the time came to stand up and walk away from the nations. It could happen very quickly or very slowly, to all of us or to most of us. It could take place in all countries or in most countries. What counts is that this exodus is now *the main and primary role* of Jewish history."[26]

---

26. Shazar, "As the Jordan River Flows from Lake Kinneret: *Jewish Science* as Redemption Science," *Orei dorot*, 389–94, here 392.

In a brilliant paraphrase of a famous saying in the lectures of the early nineteenth-century *Verein für Kultur und Wissenschaft der Juden,*[27] Shazar compared the dialectical course of Judaic Studies in European culture to the Jordan River, which flows into the Sea of Galilee without disappearing: "The Jordan [River] is not obliterated within Lake Kinneret; it retains its ancient waters, exalted waters that do not cease to be its own, even if they have neither a shore of their own nor a special appearance, neither a particular taste nor a color."[28]

Scholars of the *Wissenschaft des Judentums,* according to Shazar, used European scientific methods to make a definitive contribution to the development of Jewish national consciousness. Indeed, what seemed to motivate the historians of the *Wissenschaft* school, was the historical need to dwell among the nations in "a strong and dignified way."[29] This scientific research into Judaism, however, was undertaken with the intention of neither assimilation into the surrounding cultures nor self-abnegation. Rather, its goal was to encourage integration and involvement in these cultures without relinquishing the Jews' national legacy. Now, said Shazar, after the great rupture in Jewish–Gentile relations (the Holocaust), the time has come to convert *Wissenschaft des Judentums,* which has lost its historical necessity, into a *"Wissenschaft* of the Jewish Resurrection."[30] The Jordan River, that stream of Jewish scholarship, flowing through the waters of the nations without being obliterated, will now flow in the Jewish (socialist!) nation-state: "With ancient might it will strive onward to deliver its waters to the fields of workers that are commanded to become fields of blessing for the renascent homeland."[31]

These passionate remarks, made at the end of World War II by one of the most influential proponents of the renascent Hebrew culture in Palestine, return us to the manner in which the shapers of the new Hebrew culture portrayed the messianic movements of the early modern era. Shazar, who at the beginning of his scholarly career presented the premodern redemption movements as failed pre-Zionist movements, drew a similar analogy in his treatment of the scholars of modern Jewish Science in the era of the struggle for emancipation. Despite substantial differences, both Sabbateans and *Wissenschaft* scholars discovered and brought to the surface deep national currents, which members of previous generations could

---

27. Here Shazar was referring to the words of the Jewish German jurist Eduard Gans (1798–1839), one of the founders of the *Verein,* regarding the future of Judaic Studies (ibid., 393): "To the Jordan flowing into the Kinneret I compare thee, Israel." Gans's words go back to an ancient Jewish tradition brought forth in a midrash in Bereishit Rabba, regarding the Jordan River, whose water passes through the Galilee lake yet does not mingle with it.

28. Shazar, "As the Jordan River Flows," 393.

29. Ibid., 391.

30. Ibid., 394.

31. Ibid.

hardly fathom. In our era of modern nationalism, so the socialist Zionist historian believed, these subterranean streams would reconverge to form a mighty river of redemption.

It was Zalman Shazar's conviction that the study of history would reveal the national nature of these phenomena and that the national baggage carried by these phenomena would nourish historical study in the present. If you will, Shazar assigned a redemptive role to the critical national historian—not, perhaps, a reincarnation of the Messiah but rather of the Messiah's *"shofar"*—the herald of national redemption—and the Messiah's *"sofer"* (scribe)—the man who researches the annals of pre-nationalist redemption movements and reports his findings.[32]

In his historical studies, this Zionist intellectual, who dedicated dozens of years to the project of creating a new Jewish culture in the Land of Israel, constructed a bridge that connected the principles of Western scholarship to the vision of national redemption fashioned by the Zionist labor movement. Zalman Shazar, the Hasid from the *shtetl* who became a Marxist historian, was but one individual out of a not inconsiderable group of Zionist activists from various, even opposing, factions who succeeded in harnessing the Jewish memory of the past to a manifestly modern vision. In no small degree, the tension-ridden dialogue between religious messianism and political radicalism, which is currently intensifying in Israel, came to the Land of Israel on bridges of the type that Shazar built. After all, Jewish messianism and political radicalism have both survived well into the twenty-first century. The "Science of Judaism" has shaped Israeli culture in ways no one could think of in Berlin or St. Petersburg.

---

32. Mind the pun that exploits the similar sound of the two Hebrew words *"shofar"* (Yiddish *shoyfer*) and *"sofer"* (Yiddish *soyfer*). These two words sound just the same in the mouths of some speakers of the Lithuanian-Yiddish dialect!

7

From St. Petersburg to Zion:
The Discovery of Jewish National Music

How rich and varied is the gamut of emotions that are revealed in the folk music of the eastern European Jews. You can find everything there: spiritual distress, the troubles and worries of daily life, joy, religious enthusiasm, faith in the coming of the messiah, philosophy, humor, love, children's songs and lullabies, dreams, and wishes. What a rich and precious treasure.... The limited scope of the intervals and the typical division of phrases give many of our songs the sophisticated form of the folk song, and they are not one whit inferior to the songs of other peoples. It is from the folk songs of the Jews of eastern Europe that the voice of the people's soul emerges and rises again; a popular culture marked by the powerful vitality of the Jewish spirit bubbles up from them. These songs throb with a strong national feeling that ceaselessly demands the unity of the nation and which also harbors the nucleus of the Jewish art music that would come later. What does it matter that the minor key is the fundamental tonality of these songs, even of the merriest of dances? Could the soul of the nation ever forget the people's condition and exult in sounds that deny that feeling?[1]

This is how the Israeli composer and cellist Joachim Stutschewsky (1891–1982) described the unique character of the folk music of the eastern European Jews. He saw it as the authentic expression of what he called the "soul of the nation" and as a source for the revival of Jewish musical activity in the modern age. In fact, it was more than that—it played an important role in the development of Jewish national feeling. In what follows, therefore, I will discuss the successive stages of what can be described as the rediscovery or even invention of Jewish national music as part of the cultural project of the Jewish national movement. I will trace the rise, flourishing maturity, and waning of the musical and ethnomusicological aspect of Jewish nationalism of which the Zionist case in Eretz Israel was only one part.

---

1. Joachim Stutschewsky, *Musika yehudit* (Jewish Music) (Tel Aviv: Mordecai Newman, 1945), 27.

"Jewish national music" refers to two distinct but not necessarily sep-arate projects: a particular musical school that was active in eastern Europe, the United States, and Eretz Israel from the late nineteenth cen-tury until the second half of the twentieth century; and a branch of ethno-musicology that collects and documents Jewish musical traditions. These projects fed into each other, for the composers who sought to write Jewish national music were very frequently also ethnomusicologists who sought to document Jewish folk music.

The systematic quest for Jewish national music began with the rise of the Jewish national movement in the Russian Empire during the last decades of the nineteenth century. Jewish nationalism lagged several decades behind other national movements in central and eastern Europe, which had appeared on the scene in the first half of that century. *Hibat Tsiyon* was not born until the 1880s, and interest in a national culture as part of the national revival came even later.

Nevertheless, once Jewish intellectuals in eastern Europe turned their eye to the cultural heritage of their people, they quickly caught up with parallel developments in other nations. In the musical case, the process was so swift that much of the Jewish activity in this field was contempora-neous with that in other national cultures. For example, the systematic collection of Jewish folk tunes in eastern Europe, stirred by the Jewish national awakening, got under way just when the composers Béla Bartók and Zoltán Kodály were undertaking a similar enterprise in the Hungar-ian part of the Austro-Hungarian Empire.[2] Many Jewish musicians who belonged to the musical mainstream in the multinational empires felt estranged from the European musical heritage and so were inspired to look for their unique identity in Jewish folk melodies.

This sense of estrangement found common cause with the reaction against the strong German influence on Jewish liturgical music, which many Jewish intellectuals had condemned decades earlier. The musical acculturation of the Jews of Germany and Austria, which came as a result of the activities of the Reform movement in the Ashkenazi communities of central Europe, especially under the influence of Solomon Sulzer (1804–1890), the cantor of the New Synagogue in Vienna, caused these intellec-tuals great unease. In St. Petersburg and Moscow, the musical centers of the Russian Empire, a group of young Jewish musicians, born in the Pale of Settlement, together with a number of Jewish musicologists, raised the banner of musical revolt against the pervasive German influence.

---

2. At the beginning of the twentieth century, Béla Bartók (1881–1945), Zoltán Kodály (1882–1967), and their students recorded 4,500 phonograph cylinders' worth of folk music at a time when traditional forms of folk culture still flourished. Their ethnomusicological project covered ethnic Hungarian groups, as well as other residents of the Carpathian basin, including Romanians, Slovaks, South Slavs, Ruthenians, Germans, Jews, and Roma people.

Influenced by the prominent Russian composers of the time (including Modeste Mussorgsky and Nikolai Rimsky-Korsakov), some of whom were their teachers, they turned their attention to eastern European folk music. Their search for authentic Jewish musical traditions led them to klezmer melodies, folk songs, and liturgical chants. Some of these figures, like Joel (Yuli Dmitrievich) Engel (1868–1927), viewed the musical heritage of eastern European Jewry, especially Hasidic *niggunim*,[3] as a rich reservoir to be collected, transcribed, and reconstructed, in order to provide a source of inspiration for the renewal of Jewish national music. Others, such as Lazare Saminsky (1882–1959), found Jewish authenticity in the songs of the Jews of the Caucasus and in the melodies of Oriental Jews.

As early as in his first Russian-language musicological study, *On Jewish Music* (St. Petersburg, 1914), Saminsky asserted that the sources of Hebrew (as distinct from Jewish) melody lay in Asia, the Land of Israel, and the biblical diaspora communities (Egypt, Babylonia, Persia). According to him, as the Jews migrated farther west they also became progressively more remote from their original Hebrew musical tradition and absorbed foreign influences from European music. Nevertheless, he believed that the original tunes survived and that it was the task of the ethnomusicologist to locate the original elements that survived from the biblical period before extracting and deciphering them.

So, whether they found the authentic national sounds in Hasidic *niggunim* and folk songs from the *shtetl*, or ranged farther and mined the liturgical melodies of the Oriental Jewish communities, Engel and Saminsky shared the belief that the original Jewish tonalities were to be found buried under the foreign musical strata. Engel believed that even if the folk songs were contaminated by foreign influences, their very adoption by Jews made them part of the national heritage. For his part, Saminsky vigorously asserted that only those "old synagogue songs" strongly marked by an aura of antiquity should be winnowed out from the folk materials collected.[4] Like the early nineteenth-century pioneers of the *Wissenschaft des Judentums* in Germany of the Romantic age, who sought to distill the "idea of Judaism" from the Jewish religious literature of the centuries, the St. Petersburg musical group wanted to extract the Jewish national motif from the musical heritage of the people.

This national ethnomusicological project lasted for about fourteen years. In 1900, Joel Engel delivered a lecture about the Jewish folk song to the Russian Imperial Ethnographic Society and sparked a movement to revive this folk music. The Society for Jewish Folk Music, whose member-

---

3. A wordless melody (sg. *nigun*) that could be sung endlessly in Hasidic gatherings, often without instruments.

4. Neil W. Levin, "Joachim Stutschewsky and His Worlds," in *Joachim Stutschewsky and the Music of His World* (New York: YIVO Institute for Jewish Research, 2018), 10.

ship included several prominent Jewish composers in the Russian Empire, was founded in 1908. In 1912, Engel and his colleagues joined the An-Sky ethnographic expedition. Traveling through the small towns of the Ukraine, they gathered rich and diverse musical material that was partially arranged and published in the anthology *Jewish Folk Melodies*.[5]

The program of these composers and ethnomusicologists to link the Jewish musical heritage to the creation of a new national music soon found a partner in the Zionist cultural renaissance in Eretz Israel. In fact, the musical project became another aspect of the "Zionist ingathering project" (*mif'al ha-kinus*). This project was one of the foundation stones of the national culture that writers, historians, and folklorists sought to create in Eretz Israel on the basis of the Jewish spiritual treasures created in the diaspora. Instead of the texts, which the promoters of the national culture were collecting, reworking, and embedding in the cultural milieu emerging in Palestine, here it was the melodies and musical motifs of the various diaspora communities that were being reclaimed.

Music was thus being conceived of as part of the Jewish cultural heritage, to be collected and gathered from the sources but also to be classified, preserved, and reworked in the spirit of the modern age. The nationalist musicians sought to give the old airs a modern form in which they could be interwoven into the emerging national culture. Although the trailblazer of this enterprise in Palestine, Abraham Zvi Idelsohn (1882–1938), was not a member of the Russian group, when he began collecting Jewish melodies his ideas about music were similar to those of Saminsky. Like the latter, Idelsohn believed that the original Jewish music was to be found in the East. Starting in 1907, he transcribed and recorded the melodies sung by the various communities in Eretz Israel. His great contribution to the ingathering project was the monumental *Thesaurus of Hebrew Oriental Melodies* (Hebrew: *Otsar neginot Yisrael*).[6]

From the perspective of traditional society, the work of Engel and Idelsohn was manifestly subversive: focusing on the melodies rather than on the religious texts and rituals associated with them was a blatant act of secularization. Furthermore, the way in which almost all of the nationalist composers and performing musicians employed the traditional melodies in a modern secular national context, which included replacing the old texts, undermined the foundations of religious ritual. This was the fate, for example, of eastern European Hasidic melodies as sung by members of

---

5. Lyudmila Sholochova, "The Phonoarchive of Jewish Folklore at the Vernadsky National Library of Ukraine," trans. Illia Labunka, State Archival Service of Ukraine (Retrieved 27 October, 2017). Sholochova describes the musical project of Engel and his colleagues. This is the most up-to-date publication on that expedition. See *Jewish Folk Melodies* (St. Petersburg: Jewish Community Center of St. Petersburg, Center for Jewish Music, 2001).

6. Abraham Zvi Idelsohn, *Hebräisch-Orientalischer Melodienschatz* (Thesaurus of Hebrew Oriental Melodies), 10 vols. (Berlin and Leipzig: Breitkopf & Härtel, 1914–1932).

the Third Aliyah. Some of these melodies were arranged as art music by Engel, who arrived in Palestine in 1924, for, in addition to collecting folk music, he was also a composer, employing motifs from the musical heritage of both eastern European and Oriental Jews.

Another prominent member of the nationalist musicians group (Society for Jewish Folk Music), the composer Joseph Achron (1886–1943), has been compared to the titanic figure of Jewish culture—Hayim Naḥman Bialik, the national poet, who played a major role in the revival of the modern Hebrew language. And indeed, these two creators succeeded in assimilating ancient elements into a modern Jewish functional and contemporary language, both literary and musical.

The Jewish musicians were intensely aware of the impressive examples of art music imbued with a national spirit that had been composed in the second half of the nineteenth and the early twentieth centuries in central and eastern Europe (Bedřich Smetana and Antonín Dvořák in Bohemia, Bartók and Kodály in Hungary, Jean Sibelius in Finland, and of course the Russian example, which was closest to them). There is a great deal of similarity between these national projects and the enterprise of Engel, Saminsky, Achron, and their colleagues. For example, the musical project of Bartók and Kodály, undertaken during the same years that Engel was developing his view of Jewish national music, has a strong touch of resistance to "foreign" influence (that is, the identification of Hungarian folk melodies with the so-called Gypsy [Roma] music). Furthermore, the same idea that later foreign layers concealed the old, authentic national melodies was a fundamental element of Bartók's search for the unique musical characteristics of the songs of the Hungarian peasantry.[7]

The argument about the vitality of pure folk art as against the parasitic character of "foreign" musical strata that Gypsy musicians had added in Hungary, is also familiar in its Jewish version. In the Jewish case, the members of the St. Petersburg group were reacting to Richard Wagner's crude anti-Semitic criticism of Jewish musicians, who, he claimed, were unable to create authentic music but could only imitate and copy. In fact, Jewish musicians took this charge to heart and called for the creation of a national Jewish music based on its own sources rather than on the hegemonic German musical model. They searched for unique musical motifs that expressed Jewish identity positively—the mirror image of the anti-Semitic critics who highlighted the negative character of these motifs. The Jewish musicians agreed with the anti-Semitic critics about what Jewish music was, but they valued it while their detractors condemned it.

In less than twenty years, the pursuit of Jewish national music, born out of the ideological ferment and cultural awakening in the Russian

---

7. Béla Bartók, "Gypsy Music or Hungarian Music?," *Musical Quarterly* 33.2 (1947): 240–57.

Empire, had split into three parallel branches. The fate of these branches, which were rooted in the same cultural soil, has something to teach us about the course of Jewish cultural nationalism in general. One of them found its way to the United States, to which both Lazare Saminsky and Joseph Achron emigrated, after brief stays in Berlin and Palestine. Saminsky devoted a great part of his career to writing liturgical music for the Reform movement. He also continued to compose art music influenced by Jewish motifs (such as "Jewish Folk Songs and Dances" and "Chassidic Suite") and to publish ethnomusicological studies.[8] Joseph Achron incorporated motifs from eastern European and Middle Eastern Jewish melodies into the symphonic music he composed. He also wrote scores for non-Jewish Hollywood films. Achron, like Saminsky, composed music for the services at Temple Emanu-El in New York.

For all its importance, however, the artistic activity of these two was not the most important influence that Jewish national music had on musical life in the United States. That was shaped, to a great extent, by the capitalist entertainment market, in which Jewish composers and performers played a key role. Klezmer music, which came to the United States along with the millions of immigrants from eastern Europe beginning in the late nineteenth century, migrated from the *shtetl* to the American metropolis in a totally spontaneous fashion. In the New World it found its way into the Yiddish theater, which flourished in the early twentieth century, and from there to the English-language stage and the new mass entertainment industry (radio, movies, television). The electronic media picked up this music and made it widely available to immigrant communities across the country.

A flourishing recording industry, which began in the years after the First World War, served as a link connecting the old melodies to the American entertainment world. According to the American Jewish ethnomusicologist Mark Slobin, in the 1920s this Jewish music played the role of an identity anchor for eastern European Jewish immigrants, who were experiencing rapid cultural transition and a concomitant sense of discontinuity.

Following the decline of American Yiddish culture, a new wave of interest in klezmer music emerged in the 1970s. Today many groups perform klezmer in various arrangements, ethnomusicologists study the genre, and it is viewed as a characteristic expression of American Jewish ethnic identity. Slobin believes that "the 'diaspora' [the United States] has become the music's homeland in many ways. So, while klezmer 'should' be understood as European—and in some ways is—it is mainly an American development and is perceived that way in Europe and even in Israel."[9]

---

8. Lazare Saminsky, *Music of the Ghetto and the Bible* (New York: Bloch, 1934).

9. Mark Slobin, *Fiddler on the Move: Exploring the Klezmer World*, American Musicspheres (New York: Oxford University Press, 2000), 9.

The second branch of the national music school was transplanted from eastern Europe to Eretz Israel, where it continued to influence art music, musical education, and popular song into the 1950s. In addition to Joel Engel, who was active in Palestine for only a few years, many composers, scholars, and teachers were involved in shaping the music of Eretz Israel during the British Mandate. A shift from eastern European music to Middle Eastern Jewish melodies (and Arab music) as a source for the national artistic project was characteristic of this trend. Its most prominent representative was the composer Alexander Uriah Boskovich (1907–1964), who began his musical career in Palestine with an orchestral suite based on eastern European Jewish melodies (*The Golden Chain* [Hebrew: *Sharsheret hazahav*], 1938).

Boskovich defined Jewish music as "the expression of the Jewish spirit and mentality in sound."[10] In *The Golden Chain*, he attempted to distill the essence of Jewish melody. He used the suite form and drew his musical material from the Jewish folk songs of eastern Europe, trying to preserve their character and their spirit because he regarded them as an expression of the Jewish national spirit. In his opinion, Jewish music expressed the emotions of the Jews scattered throughout the world, claiming to share this approach to composition with Kodály and Bartók. Boskovich changed nothing in the melodic structure of the songs he drew on, which is why he referred to his music as authentic folklore.

Some years later, the same composer became one of the leading representatives of what was known as the "Mediterranean style." His *Semitic Suite*, written under the influence of Mediterranean melodies and rhythms, premiered in 1946. The imprint of Mediterranean music can also be felt in some of the works of other prominent Israeli composers active between the 1930s and 1960s. For example, Paul Ben-Haim (1897–1984) incorporated traditional Oriental melodies in his work and became one of the most influential exponents of the "Mediterranean style."

Jewish musical nationalism, in its Zionist avatar in Eretz Israel, linked biblical motifs with local forms. The pursuit of localism produced a musical parallel to the use that writers, poets, painters, and sculptors made of the landscapes of Eretz Israel and of the culture of the indigenous non-European population. But the composers had the added difficulty of trying to include non-European musical forms in compositions written in European styles for performance on Western instruments. The Israeli musicologist Jehoash Hirshberg has noted what he calls "the blurring of

---

10. Alexander Boskovitch, "A Zsido Zene Problema"(The Problem of Jewish Music), in *Kelet es Nyugat Kozott* (1937), 31; here cited from Jehoash Hirshberg, "Alexander U. Boskovitch and the Quest for an Israeli National Musical Style," in *Modern Jews and Their Musical Agendas*, ed. Ezra Mendelsohn, Studies in Contemporary Jewry 9 (New York: Oxford University Press 1993), 92–109, here 96.

the ideal of Orientalism" in art music.[11] In his view, this school made a programmatic statement but lacked a clear definition of a musical style, and there was no real contact between the creators and performers of local music, Arabs or Oriental Jews, and the composers and performers of European music.

This Mediterranean music had become the focus of ethnomusicology, in Eretz Israel by the mid-1930s in the scholarly work of Robert Lachmann (1892–1939) and his student Edith Gerson-Kiwi (1908–1992). Lachmann, the founder of the archive of recordings of Eastern and Jewish music at the Hebrew University, wrote in 1937, "I have often endeavored to explain that no proper study of traditional Jewish music is possible unless adjacent fields, the music of the Oriental Christian churches, as well as Arabic music, are studied alongside it."[12]

The third branch of the school continued its career in Russia after the Bolshevik Revolution, and the study of Jewish folk music found a place in the musical life of the Soviet Union. Of course, it followed a different course from those taken by the same Jewish music of eastern European origin either in the American free market or in the immigrant society in the Land of Israel, developing its own Hebrew national culture.

In the Soviet Union, this national music merged into the distinctive Jewish culture that survived and was even supported by the Soviet regime in the 1920s and 1930s, within the strict limitations imposed by ideology and politics. In those years, musical life, musical education, and the shaping of culture in general were gradually swallowed up by the regime and subordinated to totalitarian ideological and political systems. Jewish musicians and ethnomusicologists who had been affiliated with the St. Petersburg group at the start of the century who did not flee from Soviet Russia during the 1920s were recruited by these institutions.

Their work was diverted to place an emphasis on the popular and proletarian elements in Jewish culture (in Yiddish) and channeled into the education of the Jewish masses through song, theater music, opera, and ballet. In the 1920s and 1930s, Mikhail Gnessin (1883–1957), Mikhail Milner (1886–1953), and Alexander Krein (1883–1951)—all members of the Society for Jewish Folk Music at the start of the century—along with Engel and Saminsky, compoed works influenced by eastern European Jewish melodies. They also wrote music for Yiddish stage plays and musical hosan-

---

11. Jehoash Hirshberg, "The Vision of the East and the Heritage of the West: Ideological Trends in the Music of the *Yishuv* and Their Influence on Israeli Music in the Last Two Decades" [Hebrew], *Iyunim bitqumat Israel, Studies in Zionism, the Yishuv and the State of Israel* 14.3 (2004): 1–13, here 3.

12. Ruth Katz and Jenny Avisrat-Levin, "Missed Opportunity: Robert Lachmann and the Beginnings of Ethnomusicological Research in the Hebrew University," in *The History of the Hebrew University, Origins and Beginnings* [Hebrew], ed. Shaul Katz and Michael Heyd (Jerusalem: Magnes, 1997), 646–59, here 657.

nas celebrating the achievements of the Bolshevik regime. Some of these were relevant to the fate of the Jews after the Revolution. For example, Krein's symphonic poem *Birobidzhan* was devoted to the autonomous Jewish region in the Far East. Even some of the most important Soviet composers, including Sergei Prokofiev (1891–1953) and Dmitri Shostakovich (1906–1975), incorporated Jewish motifs in their works.

Jewish ethnomusicology in the early Soviet Union focused on aspects dictated by the regime's ideological line. For example, Soviet scholarship underscored the link between Jewish melodies and those of the peoples among whom the Jews lived; the antireligious and antiestablishment character of Jewish popular culture was highlighted; and links with contemporary ethnomusicological research being conducted outside the Soviet Union were downplayed. The bulk of the research was undertaken by the Jewish sections of the Academies of Science in Minsk (Belorussia) and Kiev (Ukraine), with much of the musical material collected by Engel and his colleagues archived in Kiev.

It was supplemented by the material collected by the *Kultur Lige* (an organization founded in Kiev in 1917/1918) and, in the Soviet period, by the ethnomusicology department of the Institute for Jewish Proletarian Culture of the Ukrainian Academy of Sciences. The work of Moisei Beregowski (1892–1961), who headed this institute between 1930 and 1948, continued the efforts of Engel and preserved diverse musical material for the future. In 1934, Beregowski published the first volume of the anthology *Jewish Musical Folklore* (in Russian and Yiddish). A collection of songs he edited with the poet Itzik Fefer, *Yidishe folks-lider (Jewish Folk Songs),* was published in Kiev in 1938. Another anthology, *Evreĭskie narodnye pesni* (also *Jewish Folk Songs),* was published in Russian in 1962. Eventually, this Soviet Jewish music would engage with the "national" Israeli and American traditions, yielding a polyphonic Jewish oeuvre that would submit to even further mixing and isolation.

This development of Jewish national music along three separate courses, in North America, Eretz Israel, and the Soviet Union, reflects the experience of eastern European Jewish culture in the twentieth century. In each venue, its fate was similar to that of Jewish languages, literature, and plastic arts in their transition from their eastern European origins to the new circumstance of the Bolshevik regime, the Yishuv in Palestine, and the urban immigrant communities in the United States. In its journey from its original home in the political and cultural context of the multinational empire, Jewish national music was transformed and modified to conform to new regimes and ideologies and adapted itself to new cultural tastes and local traditions in unfamiliar landscapes.

The fascinating cultural phenomenon of the interweaving of the very same reservoir of musical motifs into the Zionist rebirth in Eretz Israel, the project of creating a proletarian culture in the Soviet Union, and the capitalist mass culture of North America is evidence that the Jewish national culture was what Itamar Even-Zohar has called a "polysystem," in which parallel and very similar alternatives of modern Jewish identity were created and disseminated.[13]

---

13. Itamar Even-Zohar, *Polysystem Studies* (Durham, NC: Duke University Press, 1990).

Conclusion

I have chosen to conclude our journey to the forgotten roots of these multifaceted Israeli cultures with the fascinating story of how twentieth-century Jewish national music came into being. As we have seen, the yearning for the authentic Jewish national melody has led both traditionalists and revolutionaries to channel the old tunes they have discovered to modernist musical compositions of all sorts. In early twentieth-century Palestine, radical socialists and Old Yishuv Hasidim would sing the same eastern European songs, albeit with different words. Ethnomusicologists from Germany and Russia would claim traditional Yemenite dance music as the true source for Israeli cultural revival, while Tel Aviv boys and girls would proudly chant a popular Zionist Hanukkah song to George Frederick Handel's music.

Concurrent with Jewish music, previous chapters illustrated how ideology, politics, and scholarship shaped other branches of the emerging culture. However, spontaneous social and cultural factors had an enormous impact in the long run. One might think of a philharmonic concert with multiple conductors, in which the musicians, albeit with musical notations, would feel free to improvise. Consider, for example, the emergence of native Hebrew in the new agricultural colonies established in the final decades of the nineteenth century. The First Aliyah Hebraist teachers from the Russian Empire tried to revive an idiomatic Hebrew based on the Bible and Mishnah. Their pupils, who spoke Yiddish at home, heard Arabic in the street, and learned French in school, developed a novel colloquial Hebrew vernacular: an eastern European syntax—much closer to that of Russian, Polish, and/or Yiddish—with a Hebraicized Arabic and French vocabulary.

Old and new, traditional and modernist, Western and non-European merged together to create unprecedented encounters with an ancient land and a multigenerational people. It was the story of four different cultural agents that played a role in those encounters: the premodern Jewish culture(s); the local Palestinian culture; the imperial cultures with which the Jews had bonded in the modern era, either in Europe or in the

Mediterranean communities; and the new Hebrew culture on which a new native generation had been raised. The new Hebrew culture (generally identified with Tel Aviv of the British Mandate period) had been created by intellectuals, writers, journalists, and party functionaries—nearly all of whom came from two multiethnic empires on the eastern and southern fringes of Europe. As the new Hebrew culture was taking shape, the recent memories of European experiences played a highly influential role in shaping the image of the New Hebrew, that mythological hero who was supposed to supersede the eastern European (or Sephardi) exilic Jew. Alas, contrary to the nationalist utopia in Tel Aviv, that proud Hebrew City, premodern Jewish exilic traditions would survive and add unanticipated layers to the new Zionist-recommended composition. The bearers of these traditions, coupled with new immigrants from Asia and Africa who have changed the ethnodemographic composition of Israeli society in the early years of statehood, would join the heated political arena and claim an active role in conducting this polycultural concert.

Israeli multiculturalism, however, goes back even further to the late Ottoman era, much before the beginning of the new Zionist settlement project. The small Jewish Yishuv in nineteenth-century Palestine resembled several different communities in the Jewish diaspora simultaneously. It had something of the social and cultural composition of Vilnius, in the Russian Empire, where Jews faced modernity in a multiethnic and multicultural context, but was also reminiscent of the situation in Ottoman Baghdad, where Jews were making their way toward modernity under the influence of Western culture, nascent Arab nationalism, and a strong Jewish tradition. When members of modern Jewish nationalism had first come to Palestine, they began to shape a new map of the land, one that involved a European-minded reading of Israel's history. And yet, the Western-minded nationalists included in their freshly drawn maps some of the old places. Ancient concepts were revisited, reshaped and transformed into new national sites of memory. Jewish mysticism gave way to history while rabbinic scholarship was translated into European "scientific" modes. The Zionist intellectuals, who dedicated dozens of years to the project of creating a new Jewish culture in the Land of Israel, constructed a bridge that connected the principles of Western scholarship to the vision of national redemption fashioned by socialist Zionists. The "Science of Judaism" that emerged in 1819 Berlin shaped Israeli culture in ways no one in nineteenth-century Europe or in the Old Yishuv of Jerusalem could have imagined. Zalman Shazar-Rubashov, the Belarusian Hasid who became a labor historian, was but one member of an influential group of Zionist activists from various nationalist factions who succeeded in harnessing Jewish history toward a manifestly modernist vision. Those intellectuals brought to the Land of Israel the tension-ridden dialogue between

traditional messianism and political radicalism, which is currently intensifying in the Jewish State. The reciprocal relations that developed within
these various cultural systems demonstrate that modern Zionist culture
was not a unique case but only one manifestation of a broader phenomenon whose roots and whose branches can also be found far from the shores
of the Mediterranean.

Index

CPSIA information can be obtained
at www.ICGtesting.com
Printed in the USA
JSHW012145270120
3828JS00001B/29